PLAYS FOR PERFORMANCE

*A series designed for
contemporary production and study
Edited by
Nicholas Rudall and Bernard Sahlins*

PIERRE AUGUSTIN DE BEAUMARCHAIS

The Marriage of Figaro

In a New Translation and Adaptation by
Bernard Sahlins

Ivan R. Dee
CHICAGO

Library of Congress Cataloging-in-Publication Data:
Beaumarchais, Pierre Augustin Caron de, 1732–1799.
    [Mariage de Figaro. English]
    The marriage of Figaro / Pierre Augustin de
Beaumarchais : in a new translation and adaptation by
Bernard Sahlins.
        p. cm.
    ISBN 1-56663-066-5. — ISBN 1-56663-065-7 (pbk.)
    1. Barbers—Spain—Seville—Drama. I. Sahlins. Bernard.
II. Title.
PQ1956.A7E5   1994
842'.5—dc20   94-26337

INTRODUCTION
by Bernard Sahlins

There are interesting questions to ask in translating an eighteenth-century drama not as a document of record but as a viable work to be staged in the late twentieth century. Do we try to respect the original text literally, as with, say, Shakespeare, or do we take account of the storytelling modes and idioms which have meaning for our time? Certainly when it comes to narrative, the effect of and the need for certain expository lines and devices, as well as the speed of narrative pacing and the choice of what is better left unsaid, have changed in this age of television and movies. What about idiom? Does it hurt the play if we find modern equivalents for idiomatic expressions, modes of address, and sentence structures, or do we try for an eighteenth-century ambience and consistency?

What I have attempted here is a "speakable" version for this time. Fortunately, in part because it is a comedy written in prose with strong behavioral elements tempering its commedia and farce origins, and because Beaumarchais's characters still have present-day counterparts, *The Marriage of Figaro* can take our stage without fundamental adapting. Accordingly, this version largely follows the original text. Some cuts have been made, and in several instances speeches have been combined; some equivalencies have been advanced for idiomatic expressions; a few minor characters, with their lines, have been eliminated; the use of "asides" as expository devices has been curtailed.

3

Beaumarchais took an active part in staging the *Marriage* and wrote a set of directions for playing and costuming his characters. His notes are exemplary in that he stressed realism and cautioned against overacting, even for the purely comic roles. Here, for example, are some of his comments on Don Gusman Brid'oison, a role in which it would be easy to succumb to burlesque: "The actor would be making a serious error and misconstruing the role if he emphasizes its ludicrous aspects. The effectiveness of the part lies in the contrast between the solemnity of his office and the absurdity of the character, and the less overacting he does the greater will be his achievement."

Again, for Figaro himself: "The actor who plays Figaro must enter deeply into the true spirit of the character...above all he must not allow the least bit of overacting."

About the Count: "Count Almaviva must be played with great nobility. At the same time he is charming and relaxed. He is immoral, but he has good manners. Properly played he serves to bring out the best in all the other roles."

In general, it is clear that Beaumarchais's views on realistic acting and on complexity of character, as well as on the necessity for playing farce "straight," are very close to ours. This is especially important for present-day production in view of the fact that many of the strongest ironies in the work are directed at a class and court culture that no longer exists for us. These ironies are best brought out through behavioral transactions: dominance and subservience, acquiescence and defiance, respect and contempt, and so forth. Indeed, the play still lives for us because Beaumarchais wrote truly of these matters and created rich characters to enact them.

CHARACTERS

COUNT ALMAVIVA, Governor of Andalusia

THE COUNTESS, his wife

FIGARO, the Count's valet and steward of the castle

SUZANNE, the Countess's principal chambermaid and Figaro's fiancée

ANTONIO, the castle gardener, Suzanne's uncle, and Fanchette's father

FANCHETTE, Antonio's daughter

CHERUBIN, principal page to the Count

BARTHOLO, a physician from Seville

MARCELINE, court housekeeper

BAZILE, the court musician

DON GUSMAN BRID'OISON, associate justice of the district

DOUBLEHAND, clerk and secretary to Don Gusman

GRIPPE-SOLEIL, a young shepherd

A YOUNG SHEPHERDESS

Peasants, etc.

The Marriage of Figaro

ACT 1

*The castle of Agas-Frescas, three leagues from Seville.
An unoccupied room in the castle. A large armchair and
a table. Figaro is measuring the floor. Suzanne is trying a
wreath in her hair.*

FIGARO: 19 by 26.

SUZANNE: *(looking in the mirror)* Figaro!

FIGARO: *(measuring)* Hmm.

SUZANNE: This way? Or this way?

FIGARO: *(still measuring)* This way, I think.

SUZANNE: No, this way. *(looks up)* Figaro! It's our
wedding day. I'm trying to look pretty and you,
you're measuring.

FIGARO: Suzanne, love, you look...ravishing. I'm
trying to figure out where our bed goes. This
way I think.

SUZANNE: In this room?

FIGARO: This is the room the Count assigned us.

SUZANNE: I don't want this room.

FIGARO: Because?

SUZANNE: I just don't.

FIGARO: You could give a reason.

SUZANNE: Suppose I don't feel like it.

9

FIGARO: Women! Once they've hooked us...

SUZANNE: Giving a reason implies I can be wrong. Are you on my side or not?

FIGARO: What's wrong with this room? It's the most convenient room in the castle, connecting the Count's suite, here, and the Countess's, here.

SUZANNE: I will not live in this room.

FIGARO: Look! Say it's the middle of the night.... Madame rings for you. Voila! a couple of steps and you're at her side. Or the Count needs me. Ring, ring; presto, a hop and a skip and I'm in there.

SUZANNE: Very nice. Now, he's rung in the morning after he's sent you off to the next village. It's something else he wants. Voila! a couple of steps and he's at my side. Then, presto, a hop and a skip and he's in there.

FIGARO: What's this all about?

SUZANNE: Just this, dear heart. The Count, tired of seducing the neighborhood beauties, is coming home, but not to his wife: it's your fiancée he has his eye on. And for that, this room is most convenient.

FIGARO: Good God! Who told you this?

SUZANNE: His loyal go-between: my learned singing teacher in his new role as the Count's pimp.

FIGARO: Bazile! My old pal! That dog!... I'll kill him!

SUZANNE: Figaro, I suppose you think the Count's generous dowry is a reward for your merit.

FIGARO: I deserve it.

SUZANNE: How stupid clever men can be.

FIGARO: So they say.

SUZANNE: Yes, but few of them believe it.

FIGARO: I believe it, now.

SUZANNE: The Count intends to restore the old *droit du seigneur*...you know what that means?

FIGARO: Where the Lord of the Manor has the right to bed all brides of his domain on their wedding night—and sometimes after their wedding night.

SUZANNE: Exactly.

FIGARO: But he abolished that when he got married himself. Otherwise I wouldn't dream of marrying you here.

SUZANNE: He did abolish it, but now he's sorry. He intends to revive it...secretly...with your fiancée today.

FIGARO: *(rubbing his forehead)* I'm shocked. My forehead is sprouting...already.

SUZANNE: Don't rub it then....

FIGARO: Why? What will happen?

SUZANNE: ...If you had even the smallest pimple, certain gossips...

FIGARO: You're laughing at me, you witch! So, his Lordship planned a secret wedding gift! I wondered why he wanted to take me to London as his errand boy, when I'm the best chief steward he's ever had here. Now I know—it's a triple promotion: him to ambassador, me to embassy courier, you to bedroom ambassadress. While

I'd be galloping off in one direction, he'd be riding my wife in another!

SUZANNE: While you were fighting your way through rain and mud for the glory of his family, he would be increasing yours.

FIGARO: It's a nice reciprocity representing me and the King at the same time. And Bazile! I'll... No, let's play along with them: take advantage of this disgusting situation; foil them and make them pay.

SUZANNE: Intrigue and money—you're in your element now.

FIGARO: What did you expect, surrender?

SUZANNE: How about fear?

FIGARO: It's no great feat to run into danger. The trick is to turn each situation to your advantage. (*paces*) The worst strategy is to face our enemy head on. We have to be smarter than that. First we get married earlier than announced to make sure it happens. We head off Marceline, that witch who's after my body, then pocket the money and collect the presents. As for Bazile, that hypocrite...(*a bell rings*)

SUZANNE: Her ladyship is awake. She insists on being the first person to speak to me on my wedding morning.

FIGARO: Because...?

SUZANNE: They say it brings luck to neglected wives. Goodbye, dear Figaro. Take care of our little problem.

FIGARO: What about a kiss to fortify me.

SUZANNE: For today's lover? What will tomorrow's husband say about that?

(Figaro kisses her)

SUZANNE: Here. *(points to her throat which he kisses)* And here. *(points to her cleavage which he kisses)*

FIGARO: I do love you.

SUZANNE: You've been telling me that from morning to night.

FIGARO: I'm ready to prove it from night to morning.

(the bell rings again)

SUZANNE: *(blowing a kiss)* Here's your kiss back. That's enough for now.

FIGARO: Right. Just use me and throw me away.

(Suzanne exits).

FIGARO: Charming girl. I do love her. Witty, lively, clever, yet prudent....

(Marceline and Bartholo enter)

FIGARO: Doctor Bartholo—and Marceline! Good morning. What brings you to the castle, Doctor? Ah! my marriage....

BARTHOLO: *(disdainful)* Pah, sir, by no means....

FIGARO: That would be very, very generous of you....

BARTHOLO: Yes, and very, very unlikely.

FIGARO: ...Since I did destroy your plan to marry the Countess.

BARTHOLO: Have you anything else to say?

FIGARO: Yes. Are they taking care of your mule?

BARTHOLO: *(enraged)* Babbler! Leave us!

FIGARO: Doctor, you're annoyed! Men like you are rough and tough—no pity for poor animals—no more than if they were men. Goodbye, Marceline. Are you still bent on suing me?

BARTHOLO: What's that?

FIGARO: *(exiting)* She'll tell you all about it—and a lot more, I'm sure.

BARTHOLO: *(watching him go)* Always the clown: insolent, impudent...

MARCELINE: But you too never change, Doctor: humorless, mean-spirited. No wonder you lost the Countess.

BARTHOLO: Bitter as ever I see, Marceline. Anyhow, why was I sent for? Has the Count had an accident?

MARCELINE: No, Doctor.

BARTHOLO: The Countess, that deceitful bitch, is ill—please God?

MARCELINE: She is pining away.

BARTHOLO: The reason?

MARCELINE: Her husband neglects her.

BARTHOLO: Ah, he avenges me.

MARCELINE: I don't understand the Count: he's unfaithful and jealous at the same time.

BARTHOLO: Unfaithful from boredom, jealous from vanity. It's common.

MARCELINE: For instance, today he presides over Suzanne's marriage to Figaro...

14

BARTHOLO: A marriage he engineered?

MARCELINE: Not exactly, but one he would like a share in celebrating—alone with the bride.

BARTHOLO: I'm sure Figaro would be willing—for a price.

MARCELINE: Bazile claims that's not true.

BARTHOLO: Bazile! That scoundrel is here too? It's a cesspool. What's he doing here?

MARCELINE: All the mischief he can. The worst thing is his tiresome passion—for me.

BARTHOLO: You could easily end that.

MARCELINE: How?

BARTHOLO: Marry him.

MARCELINE: A crude joke. Why didn't you end our affair that way? After I bore you a son. Poor little Emmanuel. I wonder where he is now.

BARTHOLO: Did I come all the way from Seville to listen to this nonsense?

MARCELINE: All right. No more. But at least you could help me marry someone else.

BARTHOLO: With pleasure. Now what mortal, abandoned of gods and women, would that be?

MARCELINE: Figaro...

BARTHOLO: Figaro!

MARCELINE: ...lively, handsome...

BARTHOLO: That scoundrel?

MARCELINE: ...Never angry, always good-humored, living for the moment, carefree and...generous...generous as...

15

BARTHOLO: As a thief.

MARCELINE: As a lord. He's utterly charming, yet he's cruel...to me.

BARTHOLO: And his Suzanne?

MARCELINE: Sly as they come. But if you'll help me, she can't hold him.

BARTHOLO: How? This is their wedding day!

MARCELINE: It's not too late. First we'll frighten her by threatening public disclosure of the Count's offer.

BARTHOLO: Where does that get us?

MARCELINE: Shame will force her to say no to the Count. He stops the marriage, supports my claim, and I get Figaro.

BARTHOLO: You devil! I'm with you. It's a great stroke; my old mistress marries the dog who robbed me of my young mistress...

MARCELINE: And the man who wants to be happy at my expense...

BARTHOLO: And the man who stole a hundred crowns from me....

MARCELINE: What sweet revenge.

BARTHOLO: To punish a villain...

MARCELINE: To marry him, Doctor, to marry him!

(enter Suzanne carrying a hat with a wide ribbon and a dress on her arm)

SUZANNE: To marry him! Who? My Figaro?

BARTHOLO: We were saying, how fortunate he is to have someone like you.

MARCELINE: Not to mention the Count. But we won't go into that.

SUZANNE: *(curtseying)* Your servant, madam. You always have something nasty to say.

MARCELINE: *(curtseying)* And I, yours, madam. Nasty? Isn't it proper that so generous a lord should share in the pleasures he procures for his servants?

SUZANNE: Procures?

MARCELINE: That's the word I used, madam.

SUZANNE: Luckily, madam's jealousy is as strong as her claims on Figaro are weak.

MARCELINE: They would be stronger, madam, if I stooped to using your tactics.

SUZANNE: Tactics, madam, well known to ladies of your type.

BARTHOLO: *(drawing Marceline away)* Goodbye, pretty bride of our Figaro.

MARCELINE: *(curtseying)* And the Count's secret accomplice.

SUZANNE: *(curtseying)* Who holds you in the highest esteem, madam.

MARCELINE: *(curtseying)* Will madam do me the honor of adding a measure of affection?

SUZANNE: *(curtseying)* For that, madam, you may be sure of my answer.

MARCELINE: *(curtseying)* Such a pretty young lady.

SUZANNE: Pretty enough to annoy you, madam.

MARCELINE: *(curtseying)* Above all, so respectable.

SUZANNE: (curtseying) Respectable as an old maid.

MARCELINE: (outraged) Old maid! An old maid!

BARTHOLO: Marceline!

MARCELINE: Let's go, Doctor, before I lose control. Goodbye, madam. (curtseys)

(exit Bartholo and Marceline)

SUZANNE: Witch! (throws dress on chair) I don't remember what I came in for.

(Cherubin runs in)

CHERUBIN: Ah, Suzanne, I've been waiting to catch you alone.

SUZANNE: What's wrong?

CHERUBIN: You're getting married and I'm going away.

SUZANNE: What does one have to do with the other? You're just tired of being a lowly page.

CHERUBIN: Suzanne, the Count has fired me.

SUZANNE: He's done that a hundred times. You've done something silly again.

CHERUBIN: He caught me with your cousin, Fanchette, last night. We were just rehearsing for tonight's pantomime. He went into a rage. "Get out," he said, "you little—." I won't repeat what he said in front of a lady. "Get out—you—word—I want you out of this castle by tomorrow!" It's over, Suzanne. Unless the Countess can change his mind, I shall never, never see you again.

SUZANNE: See me? So it's my turn, is it? It's no longer the Countess you're secretly sighing for?

CHERUBIN: Suzanne, she's noble and beautiful—and unapproachable.

SUZANNE: Which means that I'm not, so you dare hope...

CHERUBIN: Dare? You know I'm a coward. But how lucky you are; to see her all the time, to talk to her, to dress her in the morning and undress her at night—one button at a time—Suzanne, what I would give...What's that?

SUZANNE: Alas, her lucky nightcap, and also the lucky ribbon that does up your fair godmother's hair for the night.

CHERUBIN: *(snatching the ribbon and dodging around the chair)* I'll take that. You can say it got torn, dirty, lost. Say anything.

SUZANNE: What a good-for-nothing scamp you'll be in three or four years. Give me that ribbon.

(she snatches for the ribbon and comes up with a piece of paper)

SUZANNE: What's this?

CHERUBIN: A song I wrote when my heart was breaking. Let me go, Suzanne, and as the memory of my beautiful Countess sadly fades, thoughts of you will console me.

SUZANNE: Console you! You tiny Don Juan! Do you think you're talking to that Fanchette of yours? You're caught with her, you sigh for the Countess, now you're trying your luck with me.

CHERUBIN: True. It's all true. I don't know what's come over me. Lately I have this pounding in my chest. My pulse races at the mere sight of a woman. The word "love" thrills me. My need to say "I love you" to someone is so strong that I run through the park shouting it aloud to the Countess, to you, to the trees, to the clouds, to the wind that wafts away my fleeting words. Yesterday I bumped into Marceline.

SUZANNE: You are in a bad way.

CHERUBIN: Why not? She's a woman. Woman, girl, maiden—the very words are thrilling.

SUZANNE: He's gone over the edge.

CHERUBIN: Fanchette listens to me. She's kind, not like you.

SUZANNE: What a pity. Now listen, young man. *(she grabs for the ribbon)*

CHERUBIN: *(dodging away)* No you don't—over my dead body. If that's not enough—how about a kiss? *(he chases her now)*

SUZANNE: *(dodging him)* If you come near me I'll report you to the Countess.

(Cherubin, seeing the Count enter, throws himself behind the chair)

CHERUBIN: It's all over.

SUZANNE: *(not seeing the Count)* Now what? *(seeing the Count)* Oh! *(interposes herself between the chair and the Count)*

COUNT: You're excited, Suzanne. Talking to yourself and your little heart beating away...very understandable on this day.

SUZANNE: My Lord, what is it? If anyone found you here with me...

COUNT: I would be sorry if our secret were out. Suzanne, you know my feelings for you. Bazile told you of my love. I have only a minute to tell you what I have in mind. *(sits in chair)*

SUZANNE: *(to herself)* I don't want to hear this.

COUNT: *(taking her hand)* You know the King has appointed me ambassador to London. I'm taking Figaro with me as my courier. And since it's a wife's duty to follow her husband...

SUZANNE: I don't want this, my Lord. I don't. Please let me go.

COUNT: But first tell me...

SUZANNE: You were doing all the talking.

COUNT: Yes—about wifely duties.

SUZANNE: Well then, since your Lordship rescued his own wife from Doctor Bartholo and married her—for love, since you abolished, in her honor, that dreadful *droit du seigneur*...

COUNT: To the great disappointment of the girls. Ah, Suzanne, a charming custom. If you would only come discuss it with me this evening in the garden, I would pay a heavy price for that favor....

BAZILE: *(offstage)* He's not at home, sir.

COUNT: *(rising)* Who's that?

SUZANNE: It's Bazile. This is dreadful!

COUNT: Go! Let no one in.

SUZANNE: And leave you here?

BAZILE: *(offstage)* His Lordship was with the Countess. I'll find out.

COUNT: I'll hide. Send him away quickly.

(He makes for the chair. Suzanne bars his way. He pushes her gently. She recoils and serves as a cover as Cherubin comes out the other side. The Count crouches and goes behind the chair, and Cherubin throws himself on the chair in a kneeling position. Suzanne takes the dress she is carrying, throws it over him, and stands in front of the chair.)

(enter Bazile)

BAZILE: Have you seen his Lordship, my dear?

SUZANNE: Now why would I have seen him? Goodbye.

BAZILE: *(advancing)* It happens to be Figaro who's looking for him.

SUZANNE: Then he's looking for a man who is his worst enemy, next to you.

COUNT: *(aside)* Now we'll see how loyal he is.

BAZILE: Ah! To want the best for a wife is to want the worst for her husband?

SUZANNE: Not by your corrupt principles.

BAZILE: What is the Count asking of you that you're not freely giving to Figaro? Thanks to a little ceremony, what was forbidden to you yesterday will be required tomorrow.

SUZANNE: Iniquitous...

BAZILE: Considering that marriage is the most farcical of all serious matters, I'm merely suggesting ...

SUZANNE: I know what you're suggesting. Who gave you permission to come in here?

BAZILE: Calm down, spitfire. God give you patience. Nothing will happen unless you want it to happen. But don't expect me to believe that Figaro can stand between you and the Count—especially when a certain little page...

SUZANNE: *(alarmed)* Cherubin!

BAZILE: *(imitating her)* Cherubin, who buzzes around you night and day. Only this morning he was lurking in the hall waiting to get in when I left. Now admit it.

SUZANNE: A wicked lie from a wicked man.

BAZILE: Because I keep my eyes open, I'm a wicked man. Didn't he even write a song for you?

SUZANNE: *(sarcastic)* Of course—written especially for me.

BAZILE: Unless he wrote it for the Countess. They say he can't keep his eyes off her. If you have any influence you should warn him about that. The Count would be merciless.

SUZANNE: *(exploding)* You are a monster—slandering an unfortunate child who's already in trouble with his master.

BAZILE: Did I invent it? I'm only repeating what everybody's saying.

COUNT: *(springing to his feet)* And what is everybody saying?

SUZANNE: Oh no!

BAZILE: Ah hah!

COUNT: Find him, Bazile, and drive him away.

BAZILE: I knew I shouldn't have come in.

SUZANNE: Oh no!

COUNT: She's fainting. Set her down in the chair.

SUZANNE: *(pushing Bazile away)* I don't want to sit down.

BAZILE: I'm sorry I made that joke about the page in your presence. I only did it to find out what she really thought. The truth...

COUNT: Give him fifty crowns and a horse and send him back to his family.

BAZILE: But, my Lord, because of a little joke?

COUNT: That little pervert! Yesterday I catch him with the gardener's daughter. Today...

BAZILE: With Fanchette?

COUNT: In her bedroom.

SUZANNE: Where my Lord no doubt had business as well.

COUNT: *(laughing)* I like that.

BAZILE: That's a good sign.

COUNT: No, I went there to look for Antonio, my drunkard of a gardener. I know he's your uncle, my dear, but he's still an old sot. I knock—no answer. Your cousin Fanchette appears looking embarrassed. I get suspicious. I talk. I look around. There's a curtained wardrobe near the door. Slowly, quietly, I lift the curtain *(demonstrates by lifting the dress from the chair)* and what do I see? *(Cherubin is exposed)* Ah!

BAZILE: Ah hah!

COUNT: Just like the last time.

BAZILE: Even better.

COUNT: *(to Suzanne)* Splendid, madam. Not even married yet and you're receiving my page. As for you, sir, your behavior is unforgivable. I won't allow Figaro, a man whom I love and esteem, to be the victim of such deception. Was he with you, Bazile?

SUZANNE: *(enraged)* There was no deception and no victim. He was there all the time you were talking to me.

COUNT: I hope you're lying. His worst enemy wouldn't wish that for him.

SUZANNE: He wanted the Countess to ask you to forgive him. When he came in he was so frightened he hid in the chair.

COUNT: Another lie. I sat in the chair when I came in.

CHERUBIN: Excuse me, my Lord, at that time I was standing behind it—shivering.

COUNT: Liar! I was behind it.

CHERUBIN: That's when I was in it.

COUNT: Then you were listening to everything we said!

CHERUBIN: My Lord, I did my best not to hear anything.

COUNT: I am betrayed. *(to Suzanne)* You will not marry Figaro now.

BAZILE: There's someone coming.

(enter the Countess, Figaro, Fanchette, and peasants all in white)

FIGARO: *(to the Countess)* Only you, madam, can win us this favor.

COUNTESS: *(to Count)* You see, sir, they credit me

with more influence than I have. But what they ask is not unreasonable...

COUNT: *(embarrassed)* It would have to be completely unreasonable for me not to...

FIGARO: *(aside to Suzanne)* Back me up.

SUZANNE: *(aside to Figaro)* Too late.

FIGARO: *(aside to Suzanne)* Try anyway.

COUNT: *(to Figaro)* What do you want?

FIGARO: My Lord, your servants, gratified by the abolition of a certain unjust privilege which your love for the Countess...

COUNT: The privilege is abolished. And...?

FIGARO: It's high time your noble act be publicly acclaimed. Since I myself benefit so greatly from it today, I would like my marriage to be the first celebration of it.

COUNT: You exaggerate, my friend. It was common decency. A true Spaniard achieves love by earning it, not by demanding it as his servile due—that is tyranny, and not the way of a Castilian nobleman.

FIGARO: *(holds up wreath)* This virginal wreath, sir, is a symbol of your generous act. *(takes Suzanne's hand)* May this young lady, whose honor your deed has preserved, receive it at your hands as an emblem for all future marriages, and may these verses which we sing in chorus, forever preserve your memory....

COUNT: It seems excessive...

FIGARO: Join with me, my friends.

ALL: His Lordship. His Lordship.

SUZANNE: Why avoid a tribute you so well deserve.

COUNT: *(aside)* Treacherous woman.

FIGARO: Look at her, my Lord. No more beautiful a bride will ever prove the greatness of your sacrifice.

SUZANNE: *(aside to Figaro)* Stop talking about me. Concentrate on praising him.

COUNT: *(aside)* This whole thing is a plot...

COUNTESS: My Lord, I join them. I will cherish the memory of this ceremony that symbolizes the love you once had for me.

COUNT: I still have it, madam, and I yield.

ALL: Hooray.

COUNT: *(aside)* I'm trapped. *(aloud)* But I ask that the ceremony be postponed for a short time. I have some other considerations. *(aside to Bazile)* Quick—get Marceline.

FIGARO: *(to Cherubin)* Well, young scamp! Why aren't you cheering?

SUZANNE: He's depressed. His Lordship has banished him.

COUNTESS: Sir, I ask clemency for young Cherubin.

COUNT: He doesn't deserve it.

COUNTESS: He's so young.

COUNT: Not as young as you think.

CHERUBIN: The right to pardon was not the right you abolished when you married her Ladyship.

SUZANNE: If it were, surely he would restore it now.

COUNT: *(embarrassed)* Of course.

COUNTESS: If he never abolished it, there's no need to restore it.

CHERUBIN: *(to the Count—significantly)* It's true, my Lord, my actions were unwise, but my words are always discreet.

COUNT: That's enough!

FIGARO: What does he mean by that?

COUNT: I said enough! Everybody wants him forgiven. I agree and I'll go further. I'll give him command of a company in my regiment.

ALL: Hurrah.

COUNT: On the condition that he leaves for Catalonia, now!

FIGARO: My Lord, tomorrow?

COUNT: Now!—that's my decision.

CHERUBIN: I obey.

COUNT: Say farewell to your godmother and ask her blessing.

(Cherubin goes on one knee before the Countess. He is overcome by her closeness and cannot speak.)

COUNTESS: Go, young man. Destiny calls. Be honest and brave, and remember us. We shall rejoice in your success.

(Cherubin rises and returns to his place)

COUNT: *(suspiciously)* Your Ladyship is greatly moved.

COUNTESS: Naturally. Who knows the fate of a boy thrown into such danger. He is my kinsman and my godchild.

COUNT: *(to Bazile)* You were right. *(to Cherubin)* Young man, kiss Suzanne for the last time.

FIGARO: Not the last time, your Highness. He'll come home on leave. Kiss me too, Captain. *(he embraces him)* Goodbye, my little Cherubin. You are going to a different life. By God, yes. No more hanging around all day with the girls, no more cream buns and custard tarts, no more charades and blind-man's-buff; just good soldiers, by God: weather-beaten and ragged-assed, weighed down with their muskets, right face, left face, forward march. On to glory, no flinching, no going back—unless a fiery shell hits...

SUZANNE: Stop that, it's horrible.

COUNTESS: What a prospect.

COUNT: Where is Marceline? Strange, she's not here.

FANCHETTE: She's gone to town.

COUNT: When will she be back?

BAZILE: God knows.

FIGARO: He should keep her away for good.

FANCHETTE: The Doctor was with her?

COUNT: Bartholo is here?

FANCHETTE: He was. She buttonholed him as soon as he came.

COUNT: *(to Bazile)* He couldn't have come at a better time.

FANCHETTE: She seemed to be terribly angry and kept mentioning cousin Figaro.

FIGARO: She's brooding about me and trying to upset our wedding.

COUNT: *(to Bazile)* She'll upset it yet, I promise you. *(to Countess)* Let us go in, madam. Bazile, I shall want you.

SUZANNE: *(to Figaro)* You'll be joining me?

FIGARO: Is he hooked yet?

SUZANNE: Silly boy.

(All go out. Figaro stops Cherubin and Bazile and brings them back.)

FIGARO: Now you two. The first scene is over; next, tonight's ceremonies. Let's learn our parts, otherwise we'll be like the actors who give their worst performances when the critics are there.

BAZILE: Mine is harder than you think.

FIGARO: *(gesturing behind his back as if he were coshing him)* But you can't imagine how rewarding it will be. You want Marceline?

BAZILE: Oh yes!

FIGARO: God knows why, but do as I say and she'll be yours.

CHERUBIN: Figaro, I'm leaving, remember?

FIGARO: Would you rather stay?

CHERUBIN: More than anything.

FIGARO: Keep calm. Not a word of complaint about having to go. Pack publicly. Dress for traveling. Make sure you're seen leaving on horseback. Gallop as far as the farm. Return on foot the back way; keep out of sight and leave the rest to me.

CHERUBIN: But Fanchette doesn't know her part.

BAZILE: What the devil have you been teaching her this last week? You've never left her side.

FIGARO: You've nothing to do today. Give her another lesson.

BAZILE: Be careful. Her father is angry. It's not studying you two have been doing. Cherubin, you'll get into real trouble one of these days. The pitcher can't go to the well too often, you know....

FIGARO: Another proverb.... All right, you old pedant, give us the wisdom of the ages. The pitcher goes to the well too often and what happens?

BAZILE: It gets filled.

FIGARO: (*going*) Not bad. Not too bad.

ACT 2

The Countess's bedroom. Great splendor: a bed in a recess, a desk down stage of it; a door up stage right; door to a small dressing room down stage left; door up stage to the maid's quarters; window on the other side.

(Suzanne and the Countess enter from right)

COUNTESS: He really wanted to seduce you?

SUZANNE: No, his Lordship wouldn't stoop to that with a servant. He offered to buy me.

COUNTESS: And Cherubin was there the whole time?

SUZANNE: First behind the armchair, then in it. He'd come hoping you would intercede for him.

COUNTESS: Why didn't he come to me directly? I would have helped.

SUZANNE: I told him that. He was so sad about leaving and particularly at parting from you... "Ah, Suzanne, how noble and beautiful she is, and how unapproachable."

COUNTESS: *(dreamily)* Really? I do wish he had come to me. *(to Suzanne)* So he heard all that went on, and my husband ended up saying...

SUZANNE: That if I didn't do as he asked he would support Marceline's claim against Figaro.

COUNTESS: He no longer loves me.

33

SUZANNE: Then why is he so jealous?

COUNTESS: Like all husbands, my dear—sheer pride. My only crime is that I've loved him too well. Now he is bored with my love. But I'll not let you suffer for having refused him. You shall marry your Figaro. Where is he?

SUZANNE: Arranging for the hunt.

COUNTESS: Ah, I forgot the Count is going hunting. That buys us some time.

(a knock at the door)

SUZANNE: *(opens the door)* Ah! it's Figaro. My Figaro. Do come in, my dear, her Ladyship is anxious to see you.

FIGARO: And how about you?

SUZANNE: If my Ladyship is glad, I am glad. She knows everything.

FIGARO: Your Ladyship shouldn't take this too seriously. What does it all amount to? A trifle, really. The Count finds a young woman attractive; he tries to make her his mistress. It's all very natural...

SUZANNE: Natural?

FIGARO: And now, because my fiancée refuses that great honor, he takes up Marceline's cause. Simple. Somebody spoils your plans so you retaliate by spoiling theirs. Everybody does it, and its what we're going to do too. As I said, it's natural.

COUNTESS: Figaro, aren't you treating all this a bit lightly?

FIGARO: In no way.

SUZANNE: Instead of taking our troubles to heart...

FIGARO: Isn't it enough I take them in hand? Now, we must proceed as methodically as he does. First we transform his greed for what is ours to anxiety over what is his.

COUNTESS: How?

FIGARO: It's already done, your Ladyship—a false rumor about you...

COUNTESS: About me? Are you out of your mind?

FIGARO: To control such people you start by getting their blood boiling. Women understand that very well. Once you get a man thoroughly enraged you can do what you want with him. I've arranged for Bazile to deliver an anonymous letter warning the Count that you've arranged a meeting with a handsome young man at tonight's ball.

COUNTESS: Figaro, I am a virtuous woman.

FIGARO: Madam. There are very few women with whom I would have dared take this risk—in case the story turned out to be true.

COUNTESS: I suppose I should thank you for that.

FIGARO: You must admit it's a charming picture: the Count rushing around and cursing his wife when he meant to be seducing mine? He's already confused, galloping here, searching there, and worrying to death. Our wedding day will come and go, and he will have done nothing to stop it. He won't dare to in your Ladyship's presence.

SUZANNE: No, but that old spinster Marceline will.

FIGARO: Brrr! That worries me a lot. You must send word to his Lordship that you'll meet him at dusk in the garden.

SUZANNE: That's still the plan?

COUNTESS: You're not letting her do that?

FIGARO: Of course not. I'll dress somebody else in her clothes. Then we catch the Count in the act.

SUZANNE: And who is playing me?

FIGARO: Cherubin.

COUNTESS: He's gone.

FIGARO: Maybe—maybe not. Will you leave it to me?

SUZANNE: Since it's a question of dishonesty, deception, and scurrilous intrigue, I think we can.

FIGARO: Two, three, four threads at once—knotted and tangled besides. Ah, I am a courtier born...

SUZANNE: They say it's a difficult profession.

FIGARO: Ask for the moon, take it, then ask for more—that's the whole secret.

COUNTESS: His confidence is contagious. Even I believe him.

FIGARO: That's my intention.

SUZANNE: You were saying...

FIGARO: I'll send Cherubin to you. Arrange his hair, dress him up. I'll teach him his part and then, your Lordship, dance to our tune.

(*Figaro exits*)

COUNTESS: (*compact in hand*) Suzanne, I'm a mess. And he'll be coming in...

SUZANNE: Your Ladyship doesn't mean to pardon him?

COUNTESS: *(bemused in front of her mirror)* I? I intend to scold him severely. He should be spanked...

SUZANNE: *(takes out the song)* Let's make him sing this song. He wrote it for you.

COUNTESS: For me? My hair is really impossible.

SUZANNE: We only have two curls to do again. Besides, the wild look is better for scolding.

COUNTESS: *(recovering)* What are you saying?

(enter Cherubin; he is sad)

SUZANNE: Come in, Captain. The ladies are at home.

CHERUBIN: I hate that title. It tells me I must leave...this place...a godmother, so kind.

SUZANNE: And so beautiful...

CHERUBIN: Oh yes!

SUZANNE: Oh yes! Good little man with his long, sly lashes. Come, my bluebird, sing her Ladyship your song.

COUNTESS: *(glancing at it)* May I ask for whom you wrote it?

SUZANNE: He's blushing—guilt if I ever saw it.

CHERUBIN: Is it wrong to...to love?

SUZANNE: *(shaking her fist)* I'll tell everything, you rogue.

COUNTESS: Now, now, let him sing it.

CHERUBIN: Madam, I'm so nervous.

SUZANNE: There, there, poopsy. Her Ladyship wants to hear your song and you go all modest and shy. I'll accompany you.

(*The Countess holds the manuscript, following the music. Suzanne, who has picked up a guitar, is behind the chair reading the accompaniment over the Countess's shoulder. Cherubin faces them.*)

CHERUBIN:
My horse was weary and slow
(And my heart was heavy with pain)
His head and mine both hung low
As we wandered over the plain.

As we wandered over the plain
(And my heart was heavy with pain)
My tears fell like soft summer rain
As I called my godmother in vain.

I called my godmother in vain
(And my heart was heavy with pain)
The Queen passing by asked me why
I rode with a tear in my eye.

I rode with a tear in my eye
(And my heart was heavy with pain)
I shall ne'er see my true love again.
I shall ne'er see my true love again.

COUNTESS: Innocent and—quite moving...in its way...

SUZANNE: Pure crap. Now, Captain, we prepare you for your greatest role. First, let's see if you can fit into my dress.

COUNTESS: I doubt it.

SUZANNE: He's about my height. Off with the coat. (*takes it off*)

38

COUNTESS: What if someone comes in?

SUZANNE: We're doing nothing wrong. The hair is a problem.

COUNTESS: Take one of my hats. *(Suzanne enters the dressing room offstage)* Until the ball begins, the Count won't know you're in the castle. Then we'll say you had to wait for your commission.

CHERUBIN: *(showing papers)* Unfortunately, I have my commission. Bazile gave it to me.

COUNTESS: They don't waste time, do they? *(she examines it)* They forgot the seal.

SUZANNE: *(entering with a huge hat)* What seal?

COUNTESS: On his commission.

SUZANNE: Already?

COUNTESS: That's what *I* said. You picked that hat?

SUZANNE: It's the nicest one you have. *(sitting beside the Countess—singing to Cherubin with pins in her mouth)*
Turn and face me
Dearest love...
(Cherubin kneels down and she does his hair) Madam, he looks charming.

COUNTESS: All he needs is a nice dress. God knows he's got the figure for it.

(Suzanne goes offstage taking Cherubin's cloak with her)

CHERUBIN: I'm so unhappy. *(loud knock)*

COUNTESS: Who is it?

COUNT: *(outside)* Why is the door locked?

39

CHERUBIN: Oh no! He'll kill me on the spot. *(he runs into the dressing room)*

COUNTESS: It's because I'm alone.

COUNT: Then to whom were you talking?

COUNTESS: To you. *(aside)* What a mistake, oh what a mistake.

(the Countess opens the door)

COUNT: *(suspicious)* You don't usually lock yourself in.

COUNTESS: Suzanne and I were trying on a few things. She's gone to her room.

COUNT: You look worried.

COUNTESS: Just surprised. We were talking about you and she's just gone and...

COUNT: Talking about me, were you? I came back because I was upset by this letter...handed to me as I was starting the hunt. I don't believe a word of it, of course but...

COUNTESS: Letter?

COUNT: The truth is, madam, there are some despicable gossips around. I've been warned that someone might be seeing you today—behind my back.

COUNTESS: That's ridiculous. He'd have to come in here—whoever he is—since I don't intend leaving this room until tomorrow.

COUNT: Even though Suzanne is getting married tonight?

COUNTESS: Even for that. I'm not well.

COUNT: Fortunately, Doctor Bartholo is here.

(Cherubin knocks over a chair in the dressing room)

COUNT: What's that noise?

COUNTESS: What noise?

COUNT: There's someone in that room, madam.

COUNTESS: Who?

COUNT: You tell me. I just came in.

COUNTESS: It must be Suzanne—tidying up.

COUNT: You said she went to her room.

COUNTESS: Well, she went somewhere. I assumed it was her room. I guess it wasn't.

COUNT: If it's Suzanne, why are you so upset?

COUNTESS: Upset about my maid?

COUNT: I don't know if it's about your maid, but you're certainly upset.

COUNTESS: What is certain, sir, is that you are more concerned about her than I am.

COUNT: I am so concerned, madam, that I want to see her right now.

COUNTESS: I believe that's your usual wish—but your suspicions are groundless.

(enter Suzanne up stage, unseen, carrying a dress)

COUNT: Then they're easily disposed of.

(he looks to the dressing room and calls)

COUNT: Suzanne, I order you to come out.

(Suzanne steps near the door to the alcove up stage)

COUNTESS: You are rude, sir. She's half naked. She was trying on some dresses, presents from me. She ran in there when she heard you.

COUNT: If she's afraid to be seen, at least she can be heard. Answer, Suzanne, are you there?

COUNTESS: Suzanne, I forbid you to answer. *(to Count)* This is outrageous.

COUNT: All right, if she won't answer, I'll see for myself—dressed or undressed.

COUNTESS: *(barring the door)* I may not be able to stop you anywhere else, but this is my room...

COUNT: Madam, I want to know what's going on. Since you won't give me the key, I'll have the door broken down.

(Suzanne, up stage, hides in the alcove)

COUNTESS: Go on, call your servants. Create a public scandal. Set every tongue in the castle wagging.

COUNT: Good point, madam. I'll do it myself. I'll just go get the tools. And so everything can remain as it is, you will be good enough to come with me, quietly, to avoid the scandal you're so worried about. You won't refuse me such a simple request, will you?

COUNTESS: Of course.

COUNT: *(he goes to the up-stage door, locks it, and removes the key)*...This door too—just so you can be proven right.

COUNTESS: *(aside)* A fatal move.

COUNT: Now, may I offer you my arm? *(raising his voice)* And Suzanne in the dressing room; if she'll be good enough to wait for me...

COUNTESS: Really, sir, this is despicable.

(the Count carts her off and locks the door behind him)

SUZANNE: *(runs to dressing room door)* Open up, Cherubin, quickly—it's Suzanne—come out!

CHERUBIN: *(coming out)* Suzanne. What shall I do?

SUZANNE: Go! Now! He'll be back in a minute.

CHERUBIN: How?

SUZANNE: I don't know, but if he finds you here he'll kill you, and that will be the end of all of us. Run! Tell Figaro what's happened.

CHERUBIN: *(at the window)* That's the garden. I might be able to jump...

SUZANNE: Impossible. It's a twenty-foot drop. Oh my poor mistress, and my wedding...Oh, God!

CHERUBIN: There's a flower bed down there. I've spoiled a bed or two before. Into the jaws of hell itself rather than hurt her—a kiss for luck.

(he kisses her and jumps out the window)

SUZANNE: Oh no! *(looks out the window)* He's practically out of sight already. The rascal. As nimble as he is pretty. He'll always find a woman to help him. *(remembers the situation and goes into the dressing room)*...Now, your Highness, break down the door if you want to.

(The Count and Countess return. He is carrying tools.)

COUNT: Well, it's all as we left it. Before I break down the door, would you care to open it?

COUNTESS: Sir, why are you bent on destroying our marriage? If it was love that drove you to such anger, I could forgive your behavior. But this is the violence of vanity.

43

COUNT: Love or vanity, you shall open the door or I'll...

COUNTESS: Very well, sir, I'll open it. But first you must listen...calmly.

COUNT: Then it isn't Suzanne...

COUNTESS: It's not what you think. We were preparing a joke, an innocent joke for this evening, and I swear...

COUNT: Yes, you swear...?

COUNTESS: That we had no intention of offending you—he or I.

COUNT: So it is a man!

COUNTESS: A boy, sir.

COUNT: I'll kill him.

COUNTESS: My God!

COUNT: Who is it?

COUNTESS: Young—Cherubin.

COUNT: Cherubin! The letter was right.

COUNTESS: Please don't think...

COUNT: Everywhere I go, that dammed page! Madam—open the door. The fact is, madam, you wouldn't have hidden him if there were nothing wrong in it.

COUNTESS: He was afraid you would be angry if you saw him.

COUNT: Come out, you little wretch.

COUNTESS: Don't. Your suspicions aren't justified. Don't be misled by his being undressed.

44

COUNT: Undressed!

COUNTESS: He was getting ready to dress as a woman. It was only...

COUNT: And you were going to stay in your room. Whore! Yes, you shall stay in your room—for a long time too. But first I'll take care of this scoundrel. He'll never be heard from again.

COUNTESS: He's a child. Please. I'll never forgive myself for this.

COUNT: Your concern makes his crime worse.

COUNTESS: *(holding out the key)* In the name of our love, let him alone.

COUNT: Our love! Hypocrite! *(opens the door)*. Suzanne!

SUZANNE: *(comes out laughing)* I'll kill him! I'll kill him! Kill him then, the wicked page.

COUNT: She's not alone. *(enters the dressing room)*

SUZANNE: *(to the Countess)* Pull yourself together. He's far away. Jumped out of the window.

COUNTESS: Suzanne, I'll never survive it.

COUNT: *(comes out; short silence)* Madam, you are quite an actress.

(the Countess, her handkerchief to her mouth, fighting for composure, says nothing)

SUZANNE: What about me, my Lord?

COUNT: So it was all a joke, madam—on me.

COUNTESS: And why not, sir?

COUNT: A pretty dreadful joke. May I ask the point of it?

COUNTESS: Does your folly deserve any sympathy?

COUNT: Folly? Where my honor is involved?

COUNTESS: Did I marry you to be perpetually neglected and spied on at the same time—all in the name of your honor?

COUNT: Madam, you are relentless.

SUZANNE: Madam should have let you call the servants.

COUNT: You're right. Forgive me. I haven't been myself lately. But why didn't you come out when I called—you wretch?

SUZANNE: I was getting dressed. Besides, her Ladyship told me not to—and quite right she was.

COUNT: Why don't you ask her to forgive me instead of harping on my mistakes?

COUNTESS: No, sir, this outrage is unforgivable. I shall retire to a convent. Clearly it's time I did so.

COUNT: You can't do that.

SUZANNE: It will be a sad day for everyone.

COUNTESS: I've made up my mind. Better regret than humiliation. He has offended me too deeply.

COUNT: Rosine!

COUNTESS: I'm no longer the Rosine you courted so ardently. I'm the Countess Almaviva, the sad, neglected wife you no longer love.

SUZANNE: Oh, madam...

COUNT: It was that damned letter that started it all.

COUNTESS: I didn't agree to it.

COUNT: You knew about it, then?

COUNTESS: It was that tricky Figaro.

COUNT: He was in on it?

COUNTESS: He gave it to Bazile.

COUNT: Who said he got it from a peasant. Well, my treacherous music master, you shall pay for all this.

COUNTESS: You ask forgiveness for yourself but you deny it to others. That's a man for you. If I'm to forgive you then there has to be a general pardon all around.

COUNT: It's done. But how can I apologize enough?

COUNTESS: Both sides were at fault.

COUNT: No, I'll take all the blame. Still, it's beyond me how women can so quickly and convincingly play a role. You blushed, you wept, you went pale. And you still are.

COUNTESS: I blushed at your unfounded suspicions. But men aren't sensitive enough to tell the difference between anger and embarrassment.

COUNT: And the page—nearly naked...?

COUNTESS: *(pointing to Suzanne)* Is here...which should make you happy since you're usually glad to see her.

COUNT: We men think we know something about tactics, but we're only children. Then you forgive me?

COUNTESS: Did I say that, Suzanne?

SUZANNE: I didn't hear it.

COUNT: Well then, say it now.

COUNTESS: *(giving him her hand)* Ah, Suzanne, how weak I am. Now no one will believe in a woman's anger.

SUZANNE: Well, don't we always have to give in to them in the end?

(The Count kisses his wife's hand. Figaro enters breathlessly.)

FIGARO: I heard your Ladyship was ill. I came as quickly as I could. I'm glad to see it was nothing.

COUNT: How attentive of you...

FIGARO: It's my job, sir. Now all your servants are below with violins and pipes, waiting to escort us to the altar—as soon as you give the word.

COUNT: And who will stay and look after the Countess?

FIGARO: But she isn't ill?

COUNT: No, but what about the man who is coming to visit her?

FIGARO: What man?

COUNT: The man who wrote the letter you gave to Bazile.

FIGARO: Who said that?

COUNT: If no one else had told me, you dog, your own face would accuse you of lying.

FIGARO: My face may be lying, but I'm not.

SUZANNE: My poor, dear Figaro. It's a lost cause. He's been told everything.

48

FIGARO: Told what everything?

SUZANNE: Told you wrote the letter so the Count would believe that it was the page and not me in the dressing room.

COUNT: Well?

COUNTESS: There's nothing to hide now, Figaro. The joke is over.

FIGARO: *(struggling to understand)* The joke...is over?

COUNT: Yes, over. Now what do you have to say?

FIGARO: Over? I say I wish the same for my wedding ceremony. Now if you will give the order...

COUNT: You admit you wrote the letter...

FIGARO: If the Countess wants it that way, and if it's what Suzanne wants and what you want, then that's what I want too. But if I were you, my Lord, I wouldn't believe a word of it.

COUNT: You're still lying.

COUNTESS: *(laughing)* Poor man. Do you really insist that he tells the truth? It's against his nature. My Lord, they are longing to be married. Let's go down to the ceremony.

COUNT: *(aside)* Where is that Marceline. *(to the others)* I have to at least change for the occasion.

COUNTESS: For our own servants?

(enter Antonio, half tipsy, with a broken flower pot)

COUNT: Ah, Antonio. Come in. Come in. What can I do for you?

ANTONIO: You can put bars on the windows that

open over my flowers. They throw everything down. They've just thrown a man out.

COUNT: Out of these windows?

ANTONIO: Look what they've done to my flowers.

SUZANNE: *(aside)* Trouble, Figaro...

FIGARO: My Lord, he's been drunk all morning.

ANTONIO: You're wrong. I'm hung over from yesterday.

COUNT: This man, this man, where is he?

ANTONIO: Where is he?

COUNT: Where is he?

ANTONIO: That's what I say. As your gardener I am responsible for your garden. A man comes falling into your garden. My reputation is at stake...

SUZANNE: *(aside)* Change the subject.

FIGARO: So you haven't stopped drinking.

ANTONIO: I'll never stop drinking.

COUNTESS: But what if you're not thirsty?

ANTONIO: That's all that distinguishes us from beasts, madam, drinking when we're not thirsty and making love at any time. You see...

COUNT: Enough! Answer me now or you're fired.

ANTONIO: If I were fired, do you think I would go?

COUNT: What do you mean?

ANTONIO: If you aren't smart enough to keep a good servant, I'm not stupid enough to lose a good master.

COUNT: *(shaking him)* You said someone threw a man out of this window.

ANTONIO: Right, just now, in a white shirt. And he ran off like a...

COUNT: And then?

ANTONIO: I tried to run after him, but I hit the fence so hard, this finger is still numb. I can't even move it like this. *(holds finger up and moves it)*

COUNT: You would recognize the man?

ANTONIO: Yes, I would—if I had seen him.

SUZANNE: *(to Figaro)* He didn't see him.

FIGARO: What a fuss about a flower pot. Crybaby! Look no further, my Lord, I was the man who jumped.

COUNT: You?

ANTONIO: Crybaby! Well, you've grown since then. You looked shorter and slimmer to me—more like that whippersnapper of a page.

FIGARO: I was crouching.

COUNT: Cherubin?

FIGARO: Oh, sure. I suppose he had his horse with him too—rode back from Seville just to jump out the window.

ANTONIO: I didn't say that. I didn't see no horses jumping out of the window or I would have mentioned it.

FIGARO: I was in the bedroom—in a white shirt. It was hot. I was waiting for Suzanne when I heard your Lordship's voice. I was frightened because of the letter. It was foolish of me, I admit. I jumped into the flower bed. Sprained my ankle; just a small sprain. *(rubs it)* Ouch!

ANTONIO: *(holding out a piece of paper)* Then this must be yours because it dropped out of your pocket when you fell.

(the Count snatches the paper)

FIGARO: *(aside)* Damn!

COUNT: I suppose the fright hasn't made you forget what this is or why you had it in your pocket?

FIGARO: *(feeling in his pockets)* Of course not. I have so many...waiting for answers.... *(takes out one piece of paper)* What's this, for example? Ah, a letter from Marceline—four pages: very nice too—and what's this? Could it be the petition from that poor poacher who's in jail? No, that's here. I had the inventory of the palace furniture in the other pocket....

(the Countess has glimpsed the paper the Count is holding)

COUNTESS: *(whispers to Suzanne)* It's his officer's commission.

SUZANNE: *(to Figaro)* It's his commission.

COUNT: You're a resourceful man. Can't you guess?

ANTONIO: His Lordship says can't you guess.

FIGARO: Shop shoving, you clown. Ah, I know. It must be that poor boy's commission. He gave it to me and I forgot to return it. How stupid of me. What will he do without it? I must run...

COUNT: And why would he give it to you?

FIGARO: He wanted me to do...something with it.

COUNT: There's nothing wrong with it.

COUNTESS: *(to Suzanne)* The seal.

SUZANNE: *(to Figaro)* The seal—missing.

COUNT: You're not answering.

FIGARO: Ah, I remember. There was something missing—he said it needed...

COUNT: Needed? What did it need?

FIGARO: Your seal. Of course it may not be important, but you know how those children are....

COUNT: *(angrily crumpling the paper)* All right. It's clear I'm not going to find out anything. *(turns to go)*

FIGARO: Are you going without authorizing my marriage?

(enter Marceline, Bazile, servants, and tenants)

MARCELINE: My Lord, do not authorize this. I ask for justice. He is obligated to me.

COUNT: Ah hah!

FIGARO: Obligations? What obligations?

COUNT: What's this all about, Marceline?

MARCELINE: A promise of marriage.

FIGARO: It's only an I.O.U. I borrowed money from her.

MARCELINE: On the condition that he marries me. Sir, you are the chief justice of this province.

COUNT: Present yourself before the court...here justice is done to one and all....

BAZILE: In that case, your honor, I wish to present my claim on Marceline.

53

COUNT: Your claim! Your claim! You have the nerve to come before me and talk about claims, king of fools.

ANTONIO: *(clapping his hands)* Got him the first try. Perfect description.

COUNT: Marceline. I am postponing the wedding pending the public examination of your claims, in the great hall. Bazile, trustworthy and reliable as you are, you can go into town and find my fellow judge. You can also bring back the peasant who gave you the letter.

BAZILE: Sir, I did not come to the castle to run errands.

COUNT: Then what do you come for?

BAZILE: As a teacher of organ, harpsichord, and singing, and to entertain your Lordship's guests on the guitar, at your pleasure.

GRIPPE-SOLEIL: I'll go, my Lord.

COUNT: Who are you?

GRIPPE-SOLEIL: Grippe-Soleil, your Lordship. I be herd-boy for the goats and I be here for the fireworks today. I know where all that legal lot hang out.

COUNT: Good! I like your enthusiasm. Off you go. *(to Bazile)* As for you—go with the gentleman and play your guitar for him on the way—at my pleasure.

BAZILE: I'm to go with him and play?

COUNT: That's what you're here for. Off you go or you're fired. *(he exits)*

BAZILE: How do I deal with an unstoppable force when I'm...

FIGARO: A movable object.

BAZILE: I'll go—but just to make sure of my own marriage to Marceline. *(to Figaro)* Listen, don't settle anything until I get back. *(picks up the guitar)*

FIGARO: "Don't settle anything"? Don't worry, even if you never get back. Come on, let's have a cheery song for the bride.

(He leads everyone off in a sequidilla. Bazile accompanies him and all join in.)

COUNTESS: And he really jumped out of the window?

SUZANNE: Just like that—light as a feather.

COUNTESS: And that gardener. I thought I was going to die. I couldn't think of a thing.

SUZANNE: It never showed, madam. I really learned about high society. A lady can tell lies with a straight face.

COUNTESS: Cherubin must go. If the Count finds him in the castle... I really don't think we should send him to meet the Count in the garden.

SUZANNE: Well, I'm certainly not going. Now my marriage is...

COUNTESS: Wait, suppose I went myself.

SUZANNE: You?

COUNTESS: No one else is put at risk, and the Count can hardly complain about making love to his wife. Tell him you'll be in the garden, but for heaven's sake don't tell anyone else.

SUZANNE: Not even Figaro...?

COUNTESS: No. He'll want to make his own plan ...get my mask and my cane. I've made up my mind.

(*Suzanne goes into the dressing room. The Countess sees the Cherubin's song, picks it up, then slips it into her bosom. Suzanne comes out and hands her the mask and cane.*)

COUNTESS: Remember, not a word to Figaro. I forbid it.

SUZANNE: Madam, it's a perfect scheme. It knits all the threads together and brings them to a proper ending—and whatever happens, my marriage is safe now.

(*she kisses the Countess's hand and they exit*)

(*During the intermission, servants prepare the courtroom: attorneys' benches down stage right and left, and slightly up stage center a platform where the judges sit.*)

ACT 3

The throne room (now the courtroom) of the castle. The Count is pacing.

COUNT: It was wrong¡to get rid of Bazile. No good comes from anger. There's something really funny going on. That letter about my wife's lover...the chambermaid locked up when I come...her mistress pretending to be terrified, or not pretending...a man jumping out of the window, then someone else admitting it, or claiming it was he. There's a missing link somewhere. ...And my wife...if some bastard really tried ...I'm losing control...really, when anger is in charge the imagination runs wild, as in a dream. Did that minx Suzanne give me away? Why am I obsessed with her? I wanted to give it up twenty times.... That Figaro certainly keeps me waiting ...(*Figaro appears up stage*) I must find out if he knows I'm in love with Suzanne. If she said a single word to him...

FIGARO: (*aside*) I thought so.

COUNT: (*aside*) I marry him off to the old maid while I see to the young one.

FIGARO: (*aside*) That's my wife.

COUNT: Who's that?

FIGARO: Me.

COUNT: What did you mean?

FIGARO: What do you mean, what did I mean?

COUNT: You said, your wife...

FIGARO: I was saying my wife said you wanted me.

COUNT: You're late.

FIGARO: I got dirty when I fell into the flower bed. I was changing.

COUNT: The servants in this house take longer to dress than their masters.

FIGARO: Because they have no servants to help them.

COUNT: *(probing)* I was thinking about taking you to London as my courier, but on second thought...

FIGARO: You've changed your mind.

COUNT: In the first place, you don't know English.

FIGARO: I know "God damn."

COUNT: I don't understand.

FIGARO: English is an all-purpose language. You can get along with so little of it. "God damn" gets you what you want anywhere in England. Suppose you'd like a nice chicken. You go into a tavern and do like this to the waiter, *(imitating a spit)* saying "God damn." They bring you a round of salt beef and no bread. Amazing! Or you feel like a good bottle of wine: just do this *(imitates drawing a cork).* "God damn." In they come with a foaming stein of beer. Marvelous! Or you meet a pretty wench mincing along with come-to-me eye, elbows well back, hips swinging—you give her a little pinch. "God damn." She lands one that makes you wonder what hit you; which shows she understands perfectly.

True, the English put in a few other words here and there, but obviously "God damn" is the basis of their language. So if your highness has no other reason for leaving me in Spain...

COUNT: *(aside)* He wants to come to London. She hasn't talked.

FIGARO: *(aside)* He thinks I don't know.

COUNT: Why did the Countess trick me? I'm attentive to her. I give her presents.

FIGARO: You give her presents, but you're unfaithful to her. Are we ever grateful for leftovers?

COUNT: There was a time when you told me everything.

FIGARO: I'm hiding nothing from you now.

COUNT: How much has the countess paid you for your help in this business?

FIGARO: How much did you give me for getting her out of the hands of the Doctor? Your Excellency, insulting a good servant makes him a bad servant.

COUNT: Your behavior is suspicious...

FIGARO: Only because you're suspicious of it.

COUNT: Your reputation is detestable...

FIGARO: Just suppose I'm better than my reputation. Are there many noblemen who could claim that?

COUNT: With your brains you should have a fortune by now.

FIGARO: When I look at the mob, fighting for fortune, rushing, pushing, elbowing, trampling down everyone in the way—every man for himself and the devil take the hindmost—I choose not to play that game.

COUNT: Once you were ambitious...

FIGARO: Your Excellency was kind enough to appoint me as steward of the castle, and a very pleasant life it is. It is true I'll miss some of the excitement of being the king's messenger, but I'll be happy to live out my life here—with my wife.

COUNT: What's to stop you from taking her to London?

FIGARO: As courier I would have to leave her too often.

COUNT: But with your brains and character you could go far in the service.

FIGARO: Go far with brains! Your highness is joking. Mediocrity and subservience—that's what succeeds.

COUNT: All you need is a little training in the art of politics...

FIGARO: I know that art.

COUNT: Like you know English?

FIGARO: It's easy. Pretend to know what you don't, and pretend not to know when you do. Hear what you don't understand and don't hear what you do. Promise what you cannot deliver, what you have no intention of delivering. Make a great secret of hiding what isn't there. Plead you're busy as you spend your time sharpening pencils. Speak profoundly to cover up your emptiness, encourage spies, reward traitors, tamper with seals, intercept letters, hide the ineptitude of your goals by speaking of them glowingly— that's all there is to politics, I swear. You're welcome to it. "I'd rather be with me girl," as the song says.

COUNT: *(aside)* He wants to stay. Suzanne has given me away! *(to Figaro)* And so you hope to win your case against Marceline?

FIGARO: Is it a crime to refuse an old maid while your Excellency takes all the young ones?

COUNT: *(laughing)* A judge puts his own interests aside to follow the law.

FIGARO: Easy on the strong, harsh on the weak.

COUNT: *(aside)* I see she's told him everything. He shall marry the spinster.

FIGARO: *(aside)* He thinks he has me fooled, and he hasn't learned anything.

(enter servant)

SERVANT: *(announcing)* Don Gusman Brid'oison.

COUNT: Brid'oison?

FIGARO: Your associate justice.

COUNT: Have him wait.

(exit servant)

FIGARO: Will that be all?

COUNT: Yes. Arrange the room for the hearing.

(as Figaro exits, Suzanne enters)

SUZANNE: My Lord—I beg your pardon. You seem angry.

COUNT: You came in for something, I suppose.

SUZANNE: Her Ladyship feels faint. I came to ask you for the smelling salts.

COUNT: *(handing her a phial)* Keep it for yourself. You'll soon need it.

SUZANNE: Sir, women of my station are not allowed to feel faint. It's a genteel condition found only in drawing rooms.

COUNT: But when a loving fiancée loses her young man...

SUZANNE: But if he pays Marceline the dowry you promised me...

COUNT: I promised?

SUZANNE: My Lord, I thought that's what I heard.

COUNT: Yes, if you gave me something in return.

SUZANNE: Isn't it my duty to obey your Lordship?

COUNT: Why didn't you say so before?

SUZANNE: Is it ever too late for the truth?

COUNT: Will you be in the garden this evening?

SUZANNE: Don't I walk there every evening?

COUNT: Why were you so obstinate this morning?

SUZANNE: With the page listening behind the chair?

COUNT: Quite right. I'd forgotten. But why the refusal when Bazile spoke for me?

SUZANNE: Do we need a go-between who can't keep his mouth shut?

COUNT: Right again. But there's Figaro—didn't you tell him?

SUZANNE: Of course. I tell him everything—except what he shouldn't know.

COUNT: You are charming. Let us be clear, my dear, we have an—arrangement: no rendezvous no dowry, no dowry no marriage.

SUZANNE: But no marriage also means no *droit de seigneur,* my Lord!

COUNT: Clever! I am mad about you. But your mistress is waiting for the smelling salts.

SUZANNE: *(handing back the phial)* Could I have talked to you without an excuse?

COUNT: *(trying to kiss her)* You are delicious.

SUZANNE: Someone is coming!

COUNT: *(going off)* This evening...

(enter Figaro)

FIGARO: There's a man in a hurry. What did you say to him?

SUZANNE: You can go to court now. You've just won your case.

FIGARO: *(following her off)* What are you talking about?

(Count reenters immediately)

COUNT: "You've just won your case." What a beautiful trap I was walking into. But what if he comes up with the money? *(an idea hits him)* Antonio...!

(The Count exits. Enter Brid'oison, Marceline, and Bartholo. Brid'oison wears his judicial robes. He has a slight stutter.)

MARCELINE: Justice Brid'oison, about my case...

BRID'OISON: Yes? Speak verbally. How do you plead?

BARTHOLO: No, she's the plaintiff. It's a breach-of-promise issue.

MARCELINE: Together with a loan default.

BRID'OISON: I see. Madam, why don't you pay up?

MARCELINE: No, sir, I was the lender.

BRID'OISON: Ah! I understand it now. So you want your money back.

MARCELINE: No, sir, I want him to marry me.

BRID'OISON: Ah, now I do understand—so he wants to marry you.

MARCELINE: No, sir. That's what the case is all about.

BRID'OISON: Do you think I don't understand what the case is all about?

MARCELINE: No, sir. *(to Bartholo)* We're in trouble.

BRID'OISON: Well, I'll understand it in court.

MARCELINE: Are you sure you want to try this case?

BRID'OISON: What do you think I bought a judgeship for?

MARCELINE: It's a great abuse—the sale of judgeships.

BRID'OISON: Yes, it would be better if we could get them for nothing. Whom are you suing?

(enter Figaro)

MARCELINE: This crook, sir.

FIGARO: I'm not disturbing you, am I? *(to Brid'oison)* His Lordship is on his way.

64

BRID'OISON: I've seen you somewhere before.

FIGARO: In Seville, counselor. I was in your wife's service.

BRID'OISON: When was that?

FIGARO: A little less than a year before the birth of your son, sir. The younger one, and a very handsome child too, if I may say so....

BRID'OISON: Yes. He's the best looker in the family. I hear you're up to your old tricks.

FIGARO: You are too kind, sir...it's a tiny matter....

BRID'OISON: A promise of marriage. Poor fool. Now where's my clerk?

FIGARO: Mr. Doublehand?

BRID'OISON: Yes, he's got a finger in every pie.

FIGARO: Finger! Both hands, I guarantee. Oh yes, I've seen him about the depositions, supplementary pleadings—the usual.

BRID'OISON: We have to fill out the forms...

FIGARO: Of course. Cases begin with litigants, but the forms earn the lawyer his fees.

BRID'OISON: Hmm. This young man is not as foolish as I thought. Sir, we shall see that justice prevails.

FIGARO: Sir, I rely on your integrity, even though you are a judge.

(enter the Count)

COUNT: Full robes, Master Brid'oison? This is only a domestic matter. Ordinary dress is good enough.

BRID'OISON: That's true, your Lordship, but I never judge without them. You see, no one dare laugh at a deputy magistrate in full robes.

COUNT: Let the public in.

(The door is opened. Enter Antonio, servants, peasants. The Count sits in his great chair, Brid'oison beside him, the Clerk on his stool behind a table, parties and lawyers on the side benches, Marceline and Bartholo at her side at one bench, Figaro on the other bench. During this scene the judges confer constantly. The bailiff calls out for silence often, and the proceedings are anything but controlled.)

BRID'OISON: Doublehand, call the first case.

DOUBLEHAND: Barbe-Agar-Raab-Madelaine-Nicole-Marceline de Verte-Allure, spinster *(Marceline rises and curtseys)* versus Figaro—Christian name, please?

FIGARO: Anonymous.

BRID'OISON: A-non-y-mous. What nationality is that?

FIGARO: My own.

DOUBLEHAND: Versus Anonymous Figaro. Status?

FIGARO: Gentleman.

COUNT: You, a gentleman?

FIGARO: It's possible—my unknown father could have been a prince.

COUNT: *(to Doublehand)* Proceed.

DOUBLEHAND: In the matter of an objection to the marriage of said Figaro, the plaintiff, Marceline de Verte-Allure, is represented by Dr. Bartholo. The defendant, contrary to usage and the rules

66

of law, asks the court's permission to represent himself.

FIGARO: Your honor, that usage is often an abus-age. Any client with even a little sense knows his case better than a lawyer, starting from scratch, who masks his ignorance by shouting at the top of his lungs; a lawyer who knows everything but the facts, cares nothing about ruining his client, boring the court, and putting the judges to sleep. Now I shall put the facts in a few simple words. Gentlemen...

DOUBLEHAND: Sir, you are the defendant, not the plaintiff. I call Dr. Bartholo to read the promissory note.

BARTHOLO: *(putting on his glasses)* This is a clear-cut case. *(reading)* I, the undersigned, acknowledge having received from Marceline de Verte-Allure the sum of two thousand piastres in the castle of Augas Frescas which I shall repay on demand, and I will marry her at the castle—etc. etc. etc. Signed, Figaro—just the one name. Your honors, my client's claim is for the repayment of the money and the fulfillment of the promise of marriage—with costs. Sirs, a more interesting case has not been tried since Alexander the Great promised to marry the fair Thalestris....

COUNT: Before we go on, sir, is there any dispute as to the validity of this document.

FIGARO: Absolutely. There is malice, error, and deliberate misrepresentation in that reading. It does not say "which I shall repay *and* I will marry her," but "which I shall repay at the castle *or* I will marry her," which is totally different.

67

COUNT: Does it say *and* or *or*?

BARTHOLO: It's *and*.

FIGARO: *Or.*

BRID'OISON: Doublehand, you read the thing.

DOUBLEHAND: Yes, let an expert tend to it. Let's see...hmm...Verte-Allure...repay on demand ...and...or...and/or...the word's badly written ... and there's a blot.

BRID'OISON: A blot? I know what that is.

BARTHOLO: I submit it is the copulative conjunction linking the correlative clauses: I will pay the lady *and* I will marry her.

FIGARO: And I submit it is an alternative conjunctive separating the clauses. I pay the wench *or* I marry her. As for this pedant, I'll outpedant him. If he talks Latin, I'll talk Greek and wipe the floor with him.

COUNT: There is no way to get at the truth here.

BARTHOLO: Your honors, in the interest of time I will not quibble about one word. We'll concede it was *or*.

FIGARO: Let the record show that.

BARTHOLO: No matter. You won't be saved by a miserable technicality. Let us examine the document further—*(reads)* "or I will marry her at the castle." Your honors, the actual site of this important ceremony is often the subject of serious contention between fiancees, and that was so in this case. Monsieur Figaro, for well-known reasons, *(looks significantly at the Count)* did not wish to marry her in the castle. My client thought otherwise. He is in effect saying, should I not repay her, I will marry her, not in the town, nor in the village, but I agree to marry her in the castle.

FIGARO: Ludicrous. The sense is clear. I will repay her at the castle—comma—or I will marry her; as in the phrase: the disease will kill you, comma, or the doctor will.

BARTHOLO: No comma, your honors, see for yourselves.

FIGARO: A small matter. Gentlemen, it makes no sense. If a man marries, can he be required to repay his wife?

(the judges confer in whispers)

BARTHOLO: Only a weasel would try to get off like that.

FIGARO: Is that what you call pleading your case, sir?

BARTHOLO: I'm defending this lady.

FIGARO: Then keep on talking nonsense, but cut the insults. When the law allowed third parties to plead for impassioned litigants, it never intended that those third parties could be insolent at will. You sir, are degrading a noble institution.

ANTONIO: *(indicating judges who are conferring again—to Marceline)* What are they jabbering about?

MARCELINE: Someone has got to Brid'oison, Now he's corrupting the Count. I'm losing my case.

BARTHOLO: I'm afraid you are.

FIGARO: Courage, Marceline.

(the judges have finished)

DOUBLEHAND: Silence!

COUNT: We find that the plaintiff can demand marriage only on default of payment. Defendant, the choice is yours. And...

FIGARO: I've won!

COUNT: However, since the document says, "I will pay on demand or I will marry, etc., the court requires the defendant to pay the two thousand piastres to the plaintiff or to marry her—today. *(he rises)*

FIGARO: I've lost.

ANTONIO: A wonderful judgment.

FIGARO: What's wonderful about it?

ANTONIO: You're not going to be my nephew. Bravo, my Lord.

BAILIFF: Court is adjourned.

(the courtroom starts to empty)

ANTONIO: I can't wait to tell Suzanne. *(exits)*

MARCELINE: I'm breathing again.

FIGARO: I'm suffocating.

(the Count passes)

FIGARO: You are leaving us, my Lord?

COUNT: The judgment is given.

FIGARO: But as a gentleman I am prohibited from marrying her...

BARTHOLO: You'll marry her.

FIGARO: ...without the permission of my noble parents.

BARTHOLO: Where are they? Show them to us.

FIGARO: Give me a little time. I'm this close. I've been looking for fifteen years.

BARTHOLO: The arrogant fool. He was just another abandoned child.

FIGARO: Not abandoned. Lost or stolen.

COUNT: Where's your proof?

FIGARO: My Lord, if the lace, the embroidery, and the jewels that the bandits found on me didn't prove my high birth, then maybe this tattoo is a clue. *(rolls up his sleeve)*

MARCELINE: Not a spatula on your right arm!

FIGARO: How did you know that?

MARCELINE: My God, it's he.

FIGARO: It's me, all right.

BARTHOLO: What he?

MARCELINE: Emmanuel.

BARTHOLO: You were kidnaped by gypsies?

FIGARO: Close to a castle.

BARTHOLO: *(pointing to Marceline)* Behold, your mother.

FIGARO: Foster mother?

BARTHOLO: Your natural mother.

COUNT: His mother!

FIGARO: Explain yourself.

71

MARCELINE: *(pointing to Bartholo)* Say hello to your father.

FIGARO: Oh no! Lord, take it back.

MARCELINE: Didn't your heart tell you a thousand times.

FIGARO: Never.

COUNT: His mother!

BRID'OISON: Clearly, he won't marry her now.

FIGARO: After all the times I kept myself from breaking this man's neck—today he turns out to be my father. Well, since heaven has kept me from committing a crime, accept my apologies—father. And you, mother, kiss me as maternally as you can.

(as they kiss, Suzanne comes in with a purse in her hand, followed by Antonio)

SUZANNE: Stop the marriage, my Lord. The Countess has given me the money to pay her.

COUNT: The devil take her. They're all in this conspiracy together. *(exits)*

ANTONIO: Wait a minute before you start paying.

SUZANNE: I've seen enough. Let's go, uncle.

FIGARO: *(stopping her)* No you don't. What have you seen?

SUZANNE: My own stupidity and your sleaziness.

FIGARO: Neither one.

SUZANNE: You just go ahead and marry her since you two are so affectionate.

FIGARO: Affectionate we are, but marriage is out of the question.

(Suzanne tries to leave. Figaro bars the way. She slaps him.)

SUZANNE: And you have the nerve to keep me here.

FIGARO: *(to the company)* I ask you, that's not very loving, is it? *(to Suzanne)* Before you leave us, I ask you to look at this lady.

SUZANNE: I am looking at her.

FIGARO: And what do you think of her?

SUZANNE: She's dreadful.

FIGARO: Jealousy, jealousy. It's so reliable.

MARCELINE: Come and kiss your future mother-in-law, my dear Suzanne. This terrible man who is teasing you is my son.

SUZANNE: You are his mother?

MARCELINE: That follows.

(Suzanne embraces her)

ANTONIO: Did this just happen?

FIGARO: So far as I know.

MARCELINE: My heart was drawn to him. Only my motive was wrong. Blood was calling to blood.

FIGARO: And that's why I turned you down. It wasn't that I hated you. After all, I borrowed your money.

MARCELINE: It's yours now. *(hands him the agreement)* And here's the rest of your dowry.

SUZANNE: *(handing him the purse)* And take this too.

FIGARO: Why, thank you very much.

MARCELINE: I was unhappy as a girl, about to be a miserable wife, but look, now I'm the most fortunate of mothers. Come here, children. Hug me. My happiness is complete. How I shall love you both.

FIGARO: *(touched)* Easy, mother. I've never cried before. They are tears of joy. How stupid. I felt them on my face and I tried to stop them. The hell with it. I'll laugh and cry at the same time. You don't have an experience like this twice.

(hugs Suzanne and his mother, one on either side of him)

MARCELINE: My darling.

SUZANNE: My dearest darling.

BRID'OISON: *(wiping his eyes)* I must be getting silly.

FIGARO: Fate, I defy you. Nothing can touch me with these two to protect me.

ANTONIO: Enough bull. When it comes to marrying into my family, your parents should be married first. You understand?

BARTHOLO: May my hand wither and drop off before I give it to the mother of such a fool.

ANTONIO: *(to Figaro)* In that case, my boy, save your breath.

SUZANNE: Oh, uncle!

ANTONIO: I will not give my sister's daughter to a man who has no father.

BRID'OISON: That's really foolish. We all have a father.

ANTONIO: Fiddlesticks. He'll not have her—never. *(exits)*

BARTHOLO: I suggest you find someone else to adopt you.

MARCELINE: Wait, Doctor.

FIGARO: Every fool in Spain is out to stop my marriage.

SUZANNE: Father, dear, he's your son.

MARCELINE: In talent, brains. In looks.

FIGARO: And he hasn't cost you a penny.

BARTHOLO: What about the hundred crowns he robbed me of?

MARCELINE: *(patting him)* We'll take such good care of you, papa.

SUZANNE: We'll be so loving, daddy dear.

BARTHOLO: *(weakening)* Father, papa, daddy dear. I'm even sillier than this gentleman *(indicating Brid'oison)*. I'm weak as a child. *(Marceline and Suzanne hug him)* No, no, I haven't said yes. Where is the Count?

FIGARO: Let's go and make him give the final yes. Any more of his tricks and we're back where we started.

(they exit, dragging Bartholo with them)

BRID'OISON: *(alone)* "Sillier than this gentleman." They really are a rude bunch.

75

ACT 4

A gallery with candelabra, hung with flowers and garlands. Down stage left a writing table and armchair.

FIGARO: *(arm around Suzanne)* Happy? This silver-tongued mother of mine has convinced her doctor. Like it or not, he's marrying her, and your churlish uncle has to shut his mouth. Only the Count is unhappy. Our marriage comes at the cost of his.

SUZANNE: It's so strange.

FIGARO: And amusing. We plotted to get one dowry from the Count; we already have two, no thanks to him. Your desperate rival, who was tormenting me like a fury, has turned into the kindest of mothers. Yesterday I was an orphan, today I have both my parents—not as magnificent as I would have wished them, but good enough.

SUZANNE: And none of it was what you planned.

FIGARO: Fate has done better than any of us could. As for the blind God we call love...*(he takes her in his arms)*

SUZANNE: He's the one who interests me.

FIGARO: Let me be your faithful dog that brings love to your pretty little door—and there remain for life.

SUZANNE: Love and you?

FIGARO: Me and love.

SUZANNE: And you won't look for any other doors?

FIGARO: If I do, you can take a thousand million lovers.

SUZANNE: You begin to exaggerate. Stick to the truth.

FIGARO: My truth is the truth.

SUZANNE: Rascal...there's only one truth.

FIGARO: Really? Ever since someone noticed that time turns old folly into new wisdom, that little fantasies become great realities, there have been a thousand varieties of truth. There are truths one knows but cannot speak—for not all truths can be spoken; there are truths upheld but not believed—for not all truths are acceptable; there are lovers' vows, mothers' threats, drinkers' resolutions, political promises, a salesman's word—there's no end to them. There's only one reliable truth—my love for Suzanne.

SUZANNE: I love to hear you talk nonsense. It shows how happy you are. Now let's talk about my date with the Count.

FIGARO: Forget it. It nearly cost our marriage.

SUZANNE: Then you don't want me to go?

FIGARO: If you love me, Suzanne, you'll let him go and shiver there alone; it serves him right.

SUZANNE: Good. It was much more difficult to say yes than it will be to say no.

FIGARO: Your truest truth?

SUZANNE: I'm not as clever as you. I only know one kind of truth.

FIGARO: And you love me a little?

SUZANNE: Lots and lots.

FIGARO: That's not much.

SUZANNE: What do you mean?

FIGARO: For love, even too much is not enough.

SUZANNE: There you go again. I shall love none but my husband.

FIGARO: Stick to that and you'll be a wonderful exception to the rule.

(he takes her in his arms as the Countess enters)

COUNTESS: I knew I'd find you two together. Go, Figaro, people are waiting for you. You can leave that to the future.

FIGARO: True, madam. I forgot. Well, I'll take my future with me.

COUNTESS: *(detaining Suzanne)* She'll follow in a moment. *(Figaro exits)*

COUNTESS: What time is the meeting with the Count?

SUZANNE: Madam, the meeting is off.

COUNTESS: No, but I'm taking your place in the garden. *(handing her a pen)* Write to him to arrange where.

SUZANNE: But if Figaro finds out...

COUNTESS: I'll take the responsibility. *(dictates)* "...May it be fine tonight under the chestnut trees."

SUZANNE: *(writing)* ... under the chestnut trees.

(Enter Cherubin dressed as a shepherdess, Fanchette and other girls carrying bouquets. They hand the flowers to the Countess.)

COUNTESS: Charming. I'm sorry I don't know all of you. Who is this adorable child?

SHEPHERDESS: My cousin, madam, here for the wedding.

COUNTESS: Lovely. Since I can't hold all your bouquets, I'll honor the stranger. *(takes Cherubin's bouquet and kisses him on the forehead)* She's blushing. *(to Suzanne)* Don't you think she looks like ...?

SUZANNE: To the life.

CHERUBIN: *(aside)* How I've longed for that kiss.

(enter the Count and Antonio)

ANTONIO: I tell you he's here. And he's changed clothes.... All his other clothes are in my daughter's room. Here's his cap.

(He looks down the line of girls, recognizes Cherubin, and takes off his bonnet. He puts the military cap on Cherubin's head.)

Right. There's our officer.

COUNTESS: Good heavens!

SUZANNE: The scamp.

ANTONIO: When I say he's here, he's here.

COUNT: Well, madam...

COUNTESS: I'm more surprised than you are, and just as angry.

COUNT: And this morning...?

COUNTESS: Here's the whole truth. This was all a joke planned by these young people. He had come down to my room. We had planned the practical joke these children have completed. As we were dressing him, you came in. He was frightened and ran. I was upset and everything else followed.

COUNT: Why haven't you left?

CHERUBIN: My Lord, I...

COUNT: You shall pay for this...

FANCHETTE: Please, your Lordship.

COUNT: What is it, Fanchette?

FANCHETTE: Since, whenever you come wanting to kiss me, you always say, "I'll give you anything you want if only you'll love me, my little Fanchette"...

COUNT: I say that?

FANCHETTE: Yes, my Lord. So instead of punishing Cherubin, let me marry him and I'll love you a lot.

COUNTESS: Well, sir, it's your turn. This child's confession, as naive as mine, holds a double truth. Any distress I cause you is unintentional, but your actions fully justify mine.

ANTONIO: You too, my Lord? I'll have to straighten her out as I did her mother. I know it's not much help, but as your Ladyship knows, little girls when they grow up...

COUNT: Some evil force is working against me.

(enter Figaro)

FIGARO: My Lord, if you are going to keep our young ladies, we can't start the ceremony or the dancing.

COUNT: Dancing?... after falling this morning and spraining your ankle?

FIGARO: It's still a little sore, but it's nothing. Come along now, my beauties.

COUNT: *(barring his way)* Lucky for you the flower bed was so soft...

FIGARO: Very lucky. Otherwise...

ANTONIO: *(barring his way)* But then he curled himself up as he jumped.

FIGARO: I suppose a skilled jumper would have stayed in mid-air, eh? Let's go, ladies.

ANTONIO: *(barring his way)* And all that time the page was galloping to Seville, eh?

FIGARO: Galloping—or maybe trotting.

COUNT: And you here with his commission in your pocket.

FIGARO: Of course. What's all this now? Come along, ladies.

ANTONIO: *(grabbing Cherubin)* There's one person here who can prove my future nephew is a liar.

FIGARO: Why, Cherubin!

ANTONIO: You get it now, right?

FIGARO: Right. I get it. What story is he telling?

COUNT: His story is that he was the jumper.

FIGARO: Could be—if he says so. I don't dispute what I know nothing about.

COUNT: So you and he both...?

FIGARO: Why not? Jumping can be infectious. And when you're in a rage, people would prefer to risk...

COUNT: Two at a time?

FIGARO: Two dozen at a time. What's the difference so long as no one, thank God, was hurt. *(to the women)* Are you coming or not?

COUNT: Is this some kind of burlesque?

(fanfare off)

FIGARO: Oh! The signal for the procession. Take your places, ladies. *(he offers his arm)* Suzanne...

(all exit, leaving Cherubin behind)

COUNT: The audacity! As for you, Mr. Con Man, get yourself properly dressed now! And don't let me see you for the rest of the evening.

COUNTESS: He'll be terribly bored.

CHERUBIN: Bored? A certain imprint on my forehead would compensate for a hundred years of loneliness. *(runs off)*

COUNT: Imprint?

COUNTESS: Of his first soldier's cap. Everything's a toy for children of his age. *(she starts to exit)*

COUNT: You're leaving?

COUNTESS: You know I don't feel well.

COUNT: Stay a while for the sake of your protégé.

COUNTESS: Here come the wedding parties.

COUNT: Weddings. Well, one must endure what one can't prevent.

(They sit down at one side of the stage. Enter the bridal parties to a Spanish tune. First, huntsmen with shrouded guns, then the officials and Brid'oison, peasants in holiday costume, girls with the bridal crowns. Antonio, who is giving Suzanne away, gives her his arm; Figaro gives his arm to Marceline. The Doctor brings up the rear. The peasants dance the fandango. At the same time Antonio brings Suzanne before the Count. As she kneels, he presents her with the bridal crown, the veil, and the bouquet. Two girls sing.)

GIRLS: All hail and sing the praise tonight
Of our Count who renounces a former right,
For your honor that pleasure he forgoes
And on a happy husband a virgin bride bestows.

(As she kneels, Suzanne pulls at the Count's coat and shows him a note in her down stage hand. As the Count adjusts her wreath, she gives it to him. He puts it in his pocket. Suzanne rises and curtseys. Figaro receives her from the Count and returns to the opposite side of the stage next to Marceline. The Count withdraws toward the wings. As he draws the letter from his pocket, he pricks his finger and puts it to his mouth.)

COUNT: Damn. Those women stick pins into everything.

FIGARO: *(who has seen everything, to his mother and Suzanne)* It's a love letter from some young woman. The pin has had the audacity to prick him.

(the Count reads the letter, then looks for the pin on the ground, finds it, and sticks it in his sleeve)

FIGARO: Everything that belongs to your lover is precious. See how he picks up the pin. What a strange bird he is.

84

(Suzanne nods to the Countess. Figaro brings Marceline to the Count when the ceremony is interrupted by a commotion at the door.)

GUARD: You can't come in here.

COUNT: What is it?

GUARD: It's Don Bazile plus the whole village. And he's singing.

COUNT: Let him in—alone.

COUNTESS: I would like to rest now.

COUNT: I appreciate your patience.

COUNTESS: Suzanne! She'll be back. *(they exit)*

(enter Don Bazile and Grippe-Soleil)

BAZILE: *(pointing to Grippe-Soleil)* Having proved my loyalty to the Count by entertaining this man, I now ask for justice.

GRIPPE-SOLEIL: Entertaining. I ain't in the least entertained. Those moldy old tunes...

COUNT: Well, Bazile, what do you want?

BAZILE: Only what belongs to me—Marceline.

FIGARO: How long since you looked a fool in the face, sir?

BAZILE: I'm doing it now.

FIGARO: Since my eyes are such a good mirror, read my warning: if you come anywhere near that lady...

BARTHOLO: *(laughing)* Why not hear what he has to say.

BAZILE: *(to Marceline)* Did you promise, yes or no, if

you weren't married in four years you'd give me the chance?

MARCELINE: Wasn't there a condition?

BAZILE: That if you could find your lost child I would adopt him.

ALL: He's found.

BAZILE: That's no obstacle.

ALL: Here he is.

BAZILE: This devil!

BRID'OISON: So you renounce your claims to his mother?

BAZILE: What could be worse than being the father of a scoundrel?

FIGARO: Being his son.

BAZILE: If you're considered a somebody here, then let me gladly be a nobody. *(exits)*

FIGARO: *(jumps with joy)* So in the end I'm to have my wife.

COUNT: *(aside)* And I my mistress. *(to Brid'oison)* Prepare the marriage contracts for my signature.

ALL: Hoorah!

(the Count and the peasants exit)

MARCELINE: Son, I owe you an apology. I did your wife an injustice. I thought she had an understanding with the Count, though Bazile said she rejected him.

FIGARO: You don't understand your son if you think he can be upset by the things women do. I defy the cleverest of them to make a fool of me.

MARCELINE: Very sensible. The sin of jealousy...

FIGARO: Is the child of pride or folly. I'm a calm fatalist on that point. If Suzanne ever deceives me, I pardon her in advance.

(enter Fanchette)

Ah, my little cousin is eavesdropping.

FANCHETTE: No, no, I'm not. They say it's naughty to listen.

FIGARO: True, but it's useful. People don't always tell you that.

FANCHETTE: I was looking for Suzanne.

FIGARO: And what do you want with her?

FANCHETTE: Since you're my cousin now, I'll tell you. I have a pin to give her.

FIGARO: A pin!...from whom, you little slut. At your age...*(catches himself and says gently)* I was teasing. This pin, that the Count gave you—was there a message?

FANCHETTE: He said to give this pin to Suzanne and say it's the seal for the big chestnut trees.

FIGARO: The big—?

FANCHETTE: Chestnut trees. I shouldn't have told you because he said don't let anybody see you.

FIGARO: And you must do as you were told, cousin. Fortunately, nobody has seen you. So run along on your errand. *(Fanchette exits)*

FIGARO: *(choking)* Well, it just shows—some things really are...

MARCELINE: What things?

FIGARO: Something I heard. It's killing me. That pin was the one he picked up, mother.

MARCELINE: So all your fine talk of tolerance was nothing but an inflated balloon—one little pin deflates it.

FIGARO: But...

MARCELINE: *(quoting)* "Jealousy! Oh, I'm a calm fatalist on that point. If Suzanne ever deceives me, I pardon her in advance."

FIGARO: We all say things on the spur of the moment. The most upright judge, pleading his own case, will bend the law. As for the young lady with the pin, she won't get away with it— she and her chestnuts. My marriage is close enough for me to be angry—on the other hand, there's still time to marry someone else and leave her to...

MARCELINE: A fine rush to judgment. Let's spoil everything on the merest suspicion. What proof have you that she's deceiving you and not the Count? Are you sure she'll meet him—and why? If she does, do you know what she'll say or what she'll do? I thought you had more sense.

FIGARO: *(kissing her hand)* My mother's right—as usual. I'll look before I leap. I know the meeting place. Goodbye, mother. *(exits)*

MARCELINE: Goodbye. I know as well. Now I've dealt with him, I'll see what Suzanne is up to, or rather warn her. She's such a pretty one. We poor, downtrodden women must protect each other from these proud and terrible fools— men—when personal interest doesn't make us enemies.

ACT 5

Evening. A chestnut grove in a park. Pavilions on either side. A garden seat down stage. Figaro, wearing a cloak and wide-brimmed hat, is pacing. Fanchette is at the entrance to the stage-left pavilion. Figaro sees her.

FIGARO: Fanchette!

(Fanchette rushes into the pavilion on the left)

(enter Bartholo, Bazile, Antonio, Brid'oison, Grippe-Soleil, and others)

FIGARO: Good evening, good evening, gentlemen. Are you all here?

BAZILE: Everyone you asked to come.

BARTHOLO: You look like a conspirator. What dark deeds are you planning?

FIGARO: You came to the castle for a wedding?

BRID'OISON: Certainly.

ANTONIO: We're on our way to the park for the party.

FIGARO: You needn't go any farther. Right here, under the chestnuts, we're going to celebrate the meeting of my respectable fiancée and that noble lord who wants her for himself....

BAZILE: I know what you're talking about. *(to the others)* I suggest we leave. There is a meeting. I'll tell you all about it—later.

89

BRID'OISON: *(to Figaro)* We'll come back.

FIGARO: When I call, all of you come running. I promise you'll see something interesting. *(to the servants)* Remember, do as I told you and light up the whole area or you'll wish you were dead. *(seizes Grippe-Soleil by the arm)*

GRIPPE-SOLEIL: Ow. Let go, you brute.

BAZILE: Heaven send you joy, Mr. Bridegroom.

(they exit)

FIGARO: Oh woman, woman, woman, frailty is indeed thy name. All living things must obey their instincts. Is it yours to deceive? After stubbornly refusing when I urged her to do it—at the very moment she accepted me, in the very midst of the ceremony—and he smiled when he read her note, the rogue. And I, standing by like a blockhead. No, my Lord Count, you won't have her, you shall not have her. Because you're a great nobleman you think you're a great genius. . . . Nobility, fortune, rank, position: how proud they make a man feel. What have you done to deserve such advantages? Took the trouble to be born—that's all; otherwise you're a rather ordinary man. While I, lost in the faceless crowd, have had to call on more knowledge, more calculation and skill just to survive than was needed to rule all of Spain for a century. And you dare measure yourself against me. . . . Someone's coming—it's she! No, nobody. The night's as dark as hell, and here I am playing the stupid role of jealous husband and I'm still only half married. *(sits down)* Oh, Suzanne, Suzanne, Suzanne, what torture you've brought me. There *is* someone coming. Now is the hour.

(Exits right. Enter the Countess dressed as Suzanne, Suzanne dressed as the Countess, and Marceline.)

SUZANNE: *(whispering to Countess)* Yes, Marceline said Figaro would be here.

MARCELINE: Shh! He's here.

SUZANNE: So—one eavesdrops while the other looks for me. Let's start.

MARCELINE: *(goes to pavilion where Fanchette is)* I don't want to miss a word of this.

SUZANNE: *(loudly)* Madam is shivering.

COUNTESS: *(loudly)* The evening is damp. I'm going inside.

SUZANNE: *(loudly)* If your Ladyship doesn't need me, I'll stay here for a while.

COUNTESS: You'll catch your death of cold.

SUZANNE: I'm used to it.

FIGARO: Oh yes! Her death of cold.

(Instead of going off, Suzanne hides behind the bushes opposite where Figaro is hiding. Enter Cherubin, dressed as an officer, singing.)

CHERUBIN: Alas, my heart is in pain
I shall never see my true love again.
(whispers loudly) Fanchette. Why, it's Suzanne.

(the Count appears up stage)

CHERUBIN: *(taking the Countess's hand though she tries to avoid him)* Suzanne. Charming Suzanne. I know it's you from this soft little hand and the way it trembles—and the beating of my heart.

COUNTESS: *(pulling her hand away and whispering loudly)* Go away!

CHERUBIN: Is it only pity that has brought you here to my hiding place?

COUNTESS: Figaro is coming.

COUNT: *(tentatively)* Suzanne?

CHERUBIN: Figaro doesn't frighten me. Besides, you're not waiting for him.

COUNTESS: Then who?

COUNT: *(aside)* There's someone with her.

CHERUBIN: It's the Count, you hussy, Remember, I was behind the chair and heard everything.

COUNT: It's that damned page.

FIGARO: *(aside)* And they say eavesdropping is wrong.

SUZANNE: *(aside)* That little meddling chatterbox!

COUNTESS: Please—go away.

CHERUBIN: I will for a reward; twenty kisses for you and a hundred for the Countess.

COUNTESS: You wouldn't dare!

CHERUBIN: Oh yes I would. You take her place with the Count, and I take his with you. The only loser is Figaro.

FIGARO: You'll pay for this.

(Cherubin tries to kiss the Countess. The Count steps between them and receives the kiss.)

COUNTESS: Oh, Lord!

FIGARO: *(hearing the kiss)* A nice little tramp I was going to marry.

CHERUBIN: *(feeling the Count's clothes)* It's his Lordship! *(he runs into the pavilion where Marceline and Fanchette are hiding)*

FIGARO: *(comes toward the Count)* Time to act! I...

COUNT: *(mistaking Figaro for the page)* One kiss is enough. *(hits Figaro)*

FIGARO: Ouch!

COUNT: That pays for the first.

FIGARO: *(retreating and rubbing his cheek)* Eavesdropping is not all fun.

(Suzanne laughs aloud from the other side of the stage)

COUNT: *(to the Countess, thinking he's talking to Suzanne)* Can you believe that page...? I hit him, hard, and he runs off laughing.

FIGARO: His was softer than mine.

COUNT: He turns up everywhere...but enough of this nonsense. He'll spoil the pleasure of finding you here.

COUNTESS: Did you believe I'd be here?

COUNT: After your clever message. *(takes her hand)* You're trembling.

COUNTESS: I was frightened.

COUNT: You shouldn't be deprived of a kiss just because I got his. *(he kisses her on the forehead)*

COUNTESS: What liberties.

FIGARO: *(aside)* You slut.

SUZANNE: *(aside)* Charming.

COUNT: *(takes her hands)* How soft and delicate. If only the Countess had such lovely hands.

COUNTESS: *(aside)* Can you believe this?

COUNT: Or such pretty fingers, or an arm so firm and round.

COUNTESS: What about love?

COUNT: Love is a private story of the heart: *pleasure* is the reality that brings me to you.

COUNTESS: Don't you love her anymore?

COUNT: I love her very much—but three years together makes marriage so respectable.

COUNTESS: What's missing??

COUNT: What I find in you, my beauty.

COUNTESS: Which is?

COUNT: I don't know. Variety perhaps... more mystery, some indefinable quality we call charm: an occasional rejection perhaps.... how do I know? Our wives think loving us should be enough, so they love us unceasingly—on and on and on— assuming that they do love us. They are so willing, available—always and all the time, until one day surfeit has replaced happiness.

COUNTESS: *(aside)* What a lesson!

COUNT: I've often thought, Suzanne, that if we husbands stray it's because our wives don't give enough attention to renewing the charm of possession with the spice of variety.

COUNTESS: So it's all up to them?

COUNT: *(laughing)* And not to the man? Of course. Can we change human nature? Our part is to win them—theirs...

COUNTESS: Theirs?

COUNT: Is to hold on to us. That's often forgotten.

COUNTESS: I won't forget it.

FIGARO: *(aside)* Nor will I.

SUZANNE: *(aside)* Nor I.

COUNT: There seems to be an echo. We're speaking too loudly. But none of this applies to you...so full of life and beauty. A dash of fantasy and you would be the most provoking of mistresses. *(kisses her forehead)* My Suzanne—a Castilian's word is his bond. Here is the gold I offer to repurchase my old right and for the delicious moment you're granting me. But since what you offer me is priceless, I add this diamond to wear as a token of our love.

COUNTESS: *(curtseying)* Suzanne accepts your generous gifts.

FIGARO: *(aside)* You can't get more sluttish than that.

SUZANNE: *(aside)* My, we're getting richer by the minute.

COUNTESS: I see torches.

COUNT: They're preparing for your wedding. We'll go into one of these pavilions until they pass by.

COUNTESS: Without a light?

COUNT: We're not planning to read.

FIGARO: She's really going in! I knew it! *(comes forward)*

COUNT: Who's goes there?

FIGARO: I'm not going, I'm coming.

COUNT: It's Figaro! *(flies)*

COUNTESS: I'm coming.

(she goes into the pavilion on the right while the count disappears among the trees)

FIGARO: I don't hear them. They've gone in, and that's that. You foolish husbands who hire detectives and spend months struggling with your suspicions—you should follow my example. Right off, I follow my wife, I listen, and instantly I get all the facts. No doubts, no questions. I know exactly where I stand. *(pacing)* Of course, it doesn't bother me at all. Her treachery leaves me unmoved. I've caught them—red-handed.

SUZANNE: *(moving forward in the dark—aside)* You'll pay for these suspicions. *(imitating the Countess)* Who's there?

FIGARO: Who's there! Someone who wishes he'd never been born.

SUZANNE: Why, it's Figaro.

FIGARO: Your Ladyship!

SUZANNE: Sh! Not so loud.

FIGARO: Heaven brings you here at the right time. Do you know where his Lordship is?

SUZANNE: I don't care, the ingrate—where is he?

FIGARO: And Suzanne—my virtuous, modest fiancée—do you know where she is?

SUZANNE: Not so loud.

FIGARO: *(points to the pavilion)* ... They're in there, together. I'm going to call...

SUZANNE: *(forgetting to disguise her voice)* Don't do that.

FIGARO: It's Suzanne. God damn.

SUZANNE: *(in the Countess's voice)* You seem upset.

FIGARO: Now she's trying to trick me.

SUZANNE: We must have our revenge, Figaro. *(takes his arm)* And I know only one way to do that.

FIGARO: *(eyeing her)* Really?

SUZANNE: Unlike men who have a hundred ways of...

FIGARO: Madam, the woman's way is by far the best.

SUZANNE: *(aside)* I'm going to beat him blue...

FIGARO: *(aside)* It would be a lark if before the marriage...

SUZANNE: But isn't a little love needed to add spice to this kind of revenge?

FIGARO: Yes, but sometimes love and respect dare not show themselves because of status.

SUZANNE: It's insulting for you to say that when you don't really mean it.

FIGARO: Ah, madam, I adore you. Consider the time, the place, the circumstances—and may your anger make up for my clumsy wooing.

SUZANNE: *(aside)* My hand is itching.

FIGARO: *(aside)* My heart is pounding.

SUZANNE: But sir, have you considered...

FIGARO: Oh yes, madam. I have considered...

SUZANNE: That where love and anger are concerned...

FIGARO: He who hesitates is lost. Your hand, madam.

SUZANNE: *(in her own voice—giving him a smack)* There it is.

FIGARO: Holy hell, what a clout.

SUZANNE: Yes? Well what about this one? *(she hits him again)*

FIGARO: Enough! Stop! What do you think you're doing, beating carpets?

SUZANNE: *(hitting him on each phrase)* There's one for your suspicions, and one for your revenge, and one for your treachery, and your tricks, and your insults, and all that you were going to do. You call this love—after the way you talked this morning?

FIGARO: Ah! Santa Maria! Yes, it's love all right. Oh, happiness! Oh, bliss. Oh, a hundred times happy Figaro! Don't stop, my darling. Beat me to your heart's content. But when you've beaten me black and blue, take a kind look at the luckiest man who was ever beaten by a woman.

SUZANNE: Lucky! You dog. You didn't even hesitate to try seducing the Countess, and with such a rush of convincing nonsense I forgot who I was and I was giving in.

FIGARO: And you really thought I didn't recognize your lovely voice?

SUZANNE: *(laughing)* You recognized me? That's good, very good—but not good enough.

FIGARO: Just like a woman. You beat me black and blue and you're still unforgiving. Now tell me what's going on? Why are you here, and why these clothes, which fooled me?

SUZANNE: You're really such an innocent. You

walked into the trap laid for someone else. We set out to catch one weasel and netted two.

FIGARO: So, who's catching the other fellow?

SUZANNE: His wife.

FIGARO: His wife?

SUZANNE: His wife.

FIGARO: Figaro, you're an idiot. Imagine not figuring that out. His wife! Oh the cunning—the infinite cunning of women. So the kisses I heard...

SUZANNE: Were given to his wife.

FIGARO: And the page's?

SUZANNE: To his Lordship.

FIGARO: You sure?

SUZANNE: *(raising her arm)* You're asking for another smack, Figaro.

FIGARO: *(kissing her hand)* I treasure every single one. But the Count hits harder than you do.

SUZANNE: There you go again. On your knees.

FIGARO: *(falling to his knees)* I deserve it. On my knees. I crawl. I grovel, belly to the ground.

SUZANNE: *(laughing)* The poor Count! What a lot of trouble he's gone to.

FIGARO: *(getting up)* Just to seduce his own wife.

(the Count appears up stage and goes to the pavilion on the right)

SUZANNE: Here he comes.

COUNT: *(opening the pavilion door)* Suzanne?

FIGARO: *(whispering)* He's looking for her. I thought—

SUZANNE: He hasn't recognized her.

FIGARO: Shall we finish him off? *(he kisses her)*

COUNT: A man kissing my wife! And I'm not armed. *(comes down stage)*

FIGARO: *(disguising his voice)* I didn't realize our usual meeting would come in the middle of a wedding.

COUNT: The man in the dressing room this morning!

FIGARO: But let's not allow my stupidity to interfere with our usual pleasures.

COUNT: Hell, death, damnation.

FIGARO: *(steering her toward the pavilion, whispering)* My, my. Blasphemy. *(aloud)* Let's hurry, madam, and make up for what we missed when I jumped from the window.

COUNT: *(aside)* Now we know everything.

SUZANNE: *(near the left-hand pavilion)* Before we go in, make sure we aren't followed. *(kisses Figaro's forehead)*

COUNT: *(shouting)* Revenge!

(Suzanne runs into the pavilion where Fanchette, Marceline, and Cherubin are. The Count grabs Figaro's arm.)

FIGARO: Sir!

COUNT: So, you dog, it's you, is it? Help! Help! Anyone! Help!

(enter running Brid'oison, Bazile, Bartholo, Antonio, Grippe-Soleil, and other members of the wedding party, with torches)

BARTHOLO: *(to Figaro)* You see—as soon as you gave us the signal.

COUNT: *(pointing to pavilion on left)* Brid'oison, guard that door.

BAZILE: *(whispering to Figaro)* Did you catch him with Suzanne?

COUNT: *(pointing to Figaro)* Surround that man at all costs.

BAZILE: Ah hah!

COUNT: Shut up! *(to Figaro)* Now, traitor, answer my questions.

FIGARO: What else can I do, my Lord, you control everything here— except yourself.

COUNT: Except myself!

ANTONIO: Now that's real talking.

COUNT: If I could be angrier, it would be at your calm insolence.

FIGARO: Are we soldiers to be killed for causes we know nothing of? I'd like to know why I shouldn't be calm?

COUNT: Outrageous! *(controlling himself)* So you pretend not to know. Please tell me, who is the lady you brought to the pavilion?

FIGARO: *(indicating the wrong pavilion)* This one?

COUNT: That one.

FIGARO: Oh, that one. She is the one who honors me with her affections.

BAZILE: *(astounded)* Ah hah!

COUNT: You all heard him?

BARTHOLO: We heard him.

COUNT: And has the lady any other commitments that you know of?

FIGARO: I know a certain Count was interested in her once, but she prefers me now.

COUNT: Prefers! *(controlling himself)* Well, I admit he's open about it. He admits it, gentlemen. When guilt is openly flaunted, the punishment must be the same.

(he goes into the pavilion)

ANTONIO: That's fair.

BRID'OISON: Who took who's wife?

FIGARO: Neither of us has had that pleasure.

COUNT: *(dragging someone from inside the pavilion)* Madam, all is lost. Your hour has come. How lucky that this detestable marriage...

FIGARO: Cherubin!

COUNT: The page!

BAZILE: Ah hah!

COUNT: Will someone rid me of this damn page! What were you doing in there?

CHERUBIN: Keeping out of your sight. You told me to.

COUNT: Antonio, you go in and bring out the whore who has dishonored me.

BRID'OISON: Not her Ladyship!

ANTONIO: It serves you right. You've strayed often enough, all over the countryside.

COUNT: Get her!

(Antonio goes in)

COUNT: You will see, gentlemen, that this page wasn't alone.

ANTONIO: *(dragging someone out)* Come, madam. No use begging to be left inside. Everyone knows you're in here.

FIGARO: Fanchette!

BAZILE: Ah ha!

COUNT: Fanchette!

ANTONIO: Leaping saints! That is smart of his Lordship, choosing me to show my own daughter is a troublemaker.

COUNT: How would I know she was in there? *(starts to go in)*

BARTHOLO: Allow me, your Excellency. I'm less excitable. *(he goes in)*

BRID'OISON: Quite a complicated business.

BARTHOLO: *(as he brings someone out)* There's nothing to fear, madam, I promise you...Marceline!

BAZILE: Ah hah!

FIGARO: Better and better. My mother's in on the joke.

ANTONIO: Worse and worse.

COUNT: I don't care about her. It's the Countess...

(Suzanne comes out with her fan over her face)

Ah, here she comes. Now what should be done with this odious...

(Suzanne and Figaro fall to their knees)

COUNT: There shall be no mercy.

(all fall to their knees except Brid'oison)

Not if there were a hundred of you.

(The Countess emerges from the other pavilion. She throws herself on her knees.)

COUNTESS: Allow me to add to the number.

COUNT: *(looking from Suzanne to the Countess)* What is going on?

BRID'OISON: What do you know, it's the Countess.

COUNT: What! It was you! I dare not ask forgiveness.

COUNTESS: *(rising)* You would say no, in my place. But I, for the third time today, forgive you unconditionally.

SUZANNE: *(rising)* And so do I.

MARCELINE: *(rising)* And I.

FIGARO: *(rising)* And I too. There *is* an echo here.

(all rise)

COUNT: I thought I was being clever. They treated me like a child.

COUNTESS: Learn from it, my Lord.

FIGARO: A day like this is good practice for a diplomat.

COUNT: Your letter?

SUZANNE: Her Ladyship dictated it.

COUNT: Then the reply should be made to her. *(kisses her hand)*

COUNTESS: Now all claims are to be paid. *(she gives the purse to Figaro and the diamond to Suzanne)*

SUZANNE: *(to Figaro)* Another dowry.

COUNT: *(to Cherubin)* How'd you like the smack on the ear?

CHERUBIN: What smack?

FIGARO: He got it on my ear. That's how great men dispense justice.

COUNT: You got it? What do you say to that, my dear?

COUNTESS: *(absorbed)* Yes, dear, for ever and ever.

COUNT: And you, judge, what do you think of it all?

BRID'OISON: What do I think? I'll tell you. I don't know what to think.

FIGARO: A sensible verdict.

COUNT: And you, Figaro?

FIGARO: I was poor and people despised me. I showed some talent and was disliked for it. Now, with a pretty wife and a fortune...

BARTHOLO: Everyone will be your friend.

FIGARO: Is that really so?

BARTHOLO: Yes. I know them.

FIGARO: *(to the audience)* My wife and fortune apart— you are all welcome to what I have.

ELEPHANT PAPERBACKS

American History and American Studies
Stephen Vincent Benét, *John Brown's Body*, EL10
Henry W. Berger, ed., *A William Appleman Williams Reader*, EL126
Andrew Bergman, *We're in the Money*, EL124
Paul Boyer, ed., *Reagan as President*, EL117
Robert V. Bruce, *1877: Year of Violence*, EL102
George Dangerfield, *The Era of Good Feelings*, EL110
Clarence Darrow, *Verdicts Out of Court*, EL2
Floyd Dell, *Intellectual Vagabondage*, EL13
Elisha P. Douglass, *Rebels and Democrats*, EL108
Theodore Draper, *The Roots of American Communism*, EL105
Joseph Epstein, *Ambition*, EL7
Lloyd C. Gardner, *Spheres of Influence*, EL131
Paul W. Glad, *McKinley, Bryan, and the People*, EL119
Daniel Horowitz, *The Morality of Spending*, EL122
Kenneth T. Jackson, *The Ku Klux Klan in the City, 1915–1930*, EL123
Edward Chase Kirkland, *Dream and Thought in the Business Community, 1860–1900*, EL114
Herbert S Klein, *Slavery in the Americas*, EL103
Aileen S. Kraditor, *Means and Ends in American Abolitionism*, EL111
Leonard W. Levy, *Jefferson and Civil Liberties: The Darker Side*, EL107
Seymour J. Mandelbaum, *Boss Tweed's New York*, EL112
Thomas J. McCormick, *China Market*, EL115
Walter Millis, *The Martial Spirit*, EL104
Nicolaus Mills, ed., *Culture in an Age of Money*, EL302
Nicolaus Mills, *Like a Holy Crusade*, EL129
Roderick Nash, *The Nervous Generation*, EL113
William L. O'Neill, ed., *Echoes of Revolt: The Masses, 1911–1917*, EL5
Glenn Porter and Harold C. Livesay, *Merchants and Manufacturers*, EL106
Edward Reynolds, *Stand the Storm*, EL128
Geoffrey S. Smith, *To Save a Nation*, EL125
Bernard Sternsher, ed., *Hitting Home: The Great Depression in Town and Country*, EL109
Athan Theoharis, *From the Secret Files of J. Edgar Hoover*, EL127
Nicholas von Hoffman, *We Are the People Our Parents Warned Us Against*, EL301
Norman Ware, *The Industrial Worker, 1840–1860*, EL116
Tom Wicker, *JFK and LBJ: The Influence of Personality upon Politics*, EL120
Robert H. Wiebe, *Businessmen and Reform*, EL101
T. Harry Williams, *McClellan, Sherman and Grant*, EL121
Miles Wolff, *Lunch at the 5 & 10*, EL118
Randall B. Woods and Howard Jones, *Dawning of the Cold War*, EL130

European and World History
Mark Frankland, *The Patriots' Revolution*, EL201
Lloyd C. Gardner, *Spheres of Influence*, EL131
Thomas A. Idinopulos, *Jerusalem*, EL204
Ronnie S. Landau, *The Nazi Holocaust*, EL203
Clive Ponting, *1940: Myth and Reality*, EL202

ELEPHANT PAPERBACKS

Literature and Letters
Stephen Vincent Benét, *John Brown's Body*, EL10
Isaiah Berlin, *The Hedgehog and the Fox*, EL21
Anthony Burgess, *Shakespeare*, EL27
Philip Callow, *Son and Lover: The Young D. H. Lawrence*, EL14
James Gould Cozzens, *Castaway*, EL6
James Gould Cozzens, *Men and Brethren*, EL3
Clarence Darrow, *Verdicts Out of Court*, EL2
Floyd Dell, *Intellectual Vagabondage*, EL13
Theodore Dreiser, *Best Short Stories*, EL1
Joseph Epstein, *Ambition*, EL7
André Gide, *Madeleine*, EL8
John Gross, *The Rise and Fall of the Man of Letters*, EL18
Irving Howe, *William Faulkner*, EL15
Aldous Huxley, *After Many a Summer Dies the Swan*, EL20
Aldous Huxley, *Ape and Essence*, EL19
Aldous Huxley, *Collected Short Stories*, EL17
Sinclair Lewis, *Selected Short Stories*, EL9
William L. O'Neill, ed., *Echoes of Revolt: The Masses,
    1911–1917*, EL5
Ramón J. Sender, *Seven Red Sundays*, EL11
Wilfrid Sheed, *Office Politics*, EL4
Tess Slesinger, *On Being Told That Her Second Husband Has
    Taken His First Lover, and Other Stories*, EL12
B. Traven, *The Bridge in the Jungle*, EL28
B. Traven, *The Carreta*, EL25
B. Traven, *Government*, EL23
B. Traven, *March to the Montería*, EL26
B. Traven, *The Night Visitor and Other Stories*, EL24
B. Traven, *The Rebellion of the Hanged*, EL29
Rex Warner, *The Aerodrome*, EL22
Thomas Wolfe, *The Hills Beyond*, EL16

Theatre and Drama
Robert Brustein, *Reimagining American Theatre*, EL410
Robert Brustein, *The Theatre of Revolt*, EL407
Irina and Igor Levin, *Working on the Play and the Role*, EL411
Plays for Performance:
    Aristophanes, *Lysistrata*, EL405
    Pierre Augustin de Beaumarchais, *The Marriage of Figaro*,
        EL418
    Anton Chekhov, *The Seagull*, EL407
    Fyodor Dostoevsky, *Crime and Punishment*, EL416
    Euripides, *The Bacchae*, EL419
    Georges Feydeau, *Paradise Hotel*, EL403
    Henrik Ibsen, *Ghosts*, EL401
    Henrik Ibsen, *Hedda Gabler*, EL413
    Henrik Ibsen, *The Master Builder*, EL417
    Henrik Ibsen, *When We Dead Awaken*, EL408
    Heinrich von Kleist, *The Prince of Homburg*, EL402
    Christopher Marlowe, *Doctor Faustus*, EL404
    The Mysteries: Creation, EL412
    The Mysteries: The Passion, EL414
    Sophocles, *Electra*, EL415
    August Strindberg, *The Father*, EL406